"Jesus commands us to love God with all our heart. And that's what Christine helps us to do in this penetrating and vulnerable book. I'm sure I won't be the only reader who relates to Christine's halting efforts to live joyfully for King Jesus. And I'm sure I won't be the only one encouraged by her testimony to God's faithfulness as he keeps his promises to never leave nor forsake us."

Collin Hansen, editorial director for The Gospel Coalition and author of *Blind Spots: Becoming a Courageous, Compassionate, and Commissioned Church*

"Through vulnerable stories and candid confessions, Christine's words had us nodding along. But she also gently beckoned us to evaluate our affections, giving Christ our full allegiance—the only One who can truly satisfy. These pages are truth-filled and encouraging! We're grateful for this book."

Emily Jensen and Laura Wilfer, cofounders of the Risen Motherhood ministry and coauthors of *Risen Motherhood: Gospel Hope for Everyday Moments*

"Once again, Christine has pulled up a seat, opened her heart, and welcomed us into the very front row of her tensions. In a self-sufficient, driven culture we would much rather disengage, preserve our energy, and focus more on ourselves than lean into the tensions of growing pains. She char hearts with the kingdom of Go sing our desires to please oursel od who saved our wretched sou r, and a woman familiar with the y shared with us, I am deeply convicted and challenged to rethink and re-assess my desires and priorities. This book will encourage, admonish, and lovingly remind us to realign our allegiance to King Jesus."

Elicia Horton, coauthor of *Enter the Ring: Fighting Together for a Gospel-Saturated Marriage*

"The Lord knew I needed this book. My heart is constantly at war within itself: allegiance to the world or allegiance to King Jesus? He knew I would need a timely, fresh reminder that living submitted to his loving rule is best, bringing freedom and peace to my soul. Christine is a friend, a gifted writer, and a compelling and faithful Bible teacher. And God, through Christine, has given us a gift in *With All Your Heart*."

Kristen Wetherell, author of *Fight Your Fears: Trusting God's Character and Promises When You Are Afraid* and coauthor of *Hope When It Hurts*

"*With All Your Heart* is a beautifully written call to action for the heart and mind of the believer. With her piercing transparency, sobering conviction, and hope-filled insights, Christine has provided a depth of theological richness, crafted in language we can all connect with."

Missie Branch, asst. dean of students to women, Southeastern Baptist Theological Seminary

"The greatest paradox in Christianity is that the cross of Christ is also the throne of Christ. King Jesus reigns over sin and death from this place of pain and shame. The cross and the kingdom come hand in hand. In her new book, *With All Your Heart: Living Joyfully through Allegiance to King Jesus*, Christine Hoover lays bare the human heart and the various allegiances we must surrender in order to follow King Jesus. She does this by laying down and laying bare her own heart and soul, for the sake of her King and her neighbors. From the first page to the last, with words pregnant with affection and truth, she cries out in her wilderness: 'Prepare the way for the Lord!'"

Irene Sun, author of *God Counts: Numbers in His Word and His World*

with all
your heart

Previous Books by Author

From Good to Grace
Messy Beautiful Friendship
Searching for Spring

with all your heart

LIVING JOYFULLY THROUGH ALLEGIANCE TO KING JESUS

CHRISTINE HOOVER

BakerBooks

a division of Baker Publishing Group
Grand Rapids, Michigan

Published by Baker Books
a division of Baker Publishing Group
PO Box 6287, Grand Rapids, MI 49516-6287
www.bakerbooks.com

Printed in the United States of America

Library of Congress Cataloging-in-Publication Data
Names: Hoover, Christine, author.
Title: With all your heart : living joyfully through allegiance to King Jesus / Christine Hoover.
Description: Grand Rapids : Baker Books, a division of Baker Publishing Group, 2020.
Identifiers: LCCN 2019028421 | ISBN 9780801094477 (paperback)
Subjects: LCSH: God (Christianity)—Worship and love.
Classification: LCC BV4817 .H66 2020 | DDC 248.4—dc23
LC record available at https://lccn.loc.gov/2019028421

The author is represented by the literary agency of Wolgemuth & Associates, Inc.

20 21 22 23 24 25 26   7 6 5 4 3 2 1

*To my brothers and sisters
of Charlottesville Community Church*

contents

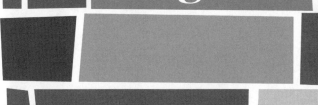

a king and

a kingdom

ONE

broken hearts

Grieved and starved.

That's how my husband, Kyle, described our current state.

We'd been tracing the back roads on a scenic loop we take when we need to be together for a few moments without the kids. Rain splashed gray against the car's windshield, mirroring the dejection we'd been laboring to diagnose in ourselves.

His words found their landing, and I knew them as true so deep inside that I instinctively doubled over into a wailing sob. My hands flew to my face, seeking to muffle the sound, as if by doing so I might stuff the emotions back inside or somehow hide they were there at all.

Grieved and starved.

Grieved, because after ten years of church planting, shepherding, cultivating deep relationships, and creating spaces for others to develop community among themselves, many of our closest friends had moved away, and we felt alone.

Starved, because we didn't merely feel alone; we also felt needy. We hungered and thirsted for even a crumb of encouragement or a caring gesture, or perhaps a break from the needs of others in order to experience renewal ourselves.

I'd felt the clouds hanging over me for weeks, as had my husband, and for both of us to be discouraged at the same time was unusual. The depth to which I'd felt it was also unusual, and I'd waited and prayed for the clouds to pass—but, as was made apparent by my uncontainable emotional outburst, I still hadn't been able to fully admit the extent of my pain or how scared I felt, knowing my typically stalwart husband was hurting as well.

I didn't want to admit the extent of my pain, because like most people I want to avoid sadness at all costs. But there was something else—something sinister—laced in the sadness, and I'd known its presence all along.

Bitterness and rage were fueling me.

I'd tucked this truth in tight, hiding what I didn't want to name and certainly didn't want others to see. I'd called it more acceptable terms, like *weariness* and *uncertainty*, which gave me permission to retreat from others, hoping even as I retreated that they might notice and laud the amount of service and ministry that had led me to such a point. These terms not only permitted my retreat from people but also permitted my retreat far from the conviction of God.

I convinced myself my primary problem was that I was not setting good boundaries, managing my time well, or saying no often enough. I'd worn myself down doing good, so perhaps I simply needed rest and an appreciative pat on the back. According to my own calculations, I'd done enough to last a long while. And so I set about looking for ways to hoard more of my energy, skills, and time for what mattered most to me. In the name of Jesus, of course.

Yet there, on the winding road, rain pounding on the glass, I cried over my hungry heart.

It became instantly clear that no amount of scheduling, control, rest, or service had fed me, because my sole motivation—this sinister, subterranean craving—had been a grasping—a yearning—for love from people. I'd set my heart on accolades and performed like a circus animal, expecting the ovation at the conclusion of the show.

My heart, clearly, was misaligned. I was working against the way and work of God in my own life, because my heart had become distorted in its search for self-glory.

Just a few minutes prior, I'd said to Kyle, "I feel like a vending machine that requires no payment. Everyone comes and pushes buttons without putting money in, and I have to respond according to their demands." I'd said this with disdain for those expecting goods and services from me, not realizing how this analogy laid my own soul bare. *Have to respond.* Those were the incriminating words, as if to *not* respond in the way others wanted wasn't even an option.

And in my line of thinking it wasn't, because I wanted to be loved.

I couldn't disappoint because I wanted to be loved.

I served because I wanted to be loved.

Though I resented everyone lined up at my vending machine, I also, in my distortion, "needed" them. I needed them to see what I did for them so they might admire and stroke me. I needed them to feed my starving soul. I felt entitled to their love, sure they should honor me in the specific ways I secretly held as firm and unrealistic expectations.

And they hadn't given me my craving, so I'd raged quietly inside, cherishing my bitterness.

I'd been looking for a way to blame others or even God himself for my "weariness" and "uncertainty," but the accusing finger only pointed back at me.

Grieved and starved, yes, but ultimately it'd been by my own hand.

At the core of my heart was an allegiance to love, but because it was an allegiance to the imperfect and incomplete love of people rather than the perfect and complete love of God, my life had become tinged with fear. Fear drove me from bed every morning and worked me into exhaustion. Fear used me up, muddied my relationships, confused my thinking, and nursed my bitterness. Fear wondered aloud if I could ever be loved for who I was rather than what I did for others, and fear made me restless in my own skin. My allegiance to the love of others broke my heart of its ability to contain and experience joy.

I had become confused about the kingdom of God.

Our Hearts Are Made for Allegiance

In our evangelical Christian culture today, we've not simply become confused about the kingdom of God; we've mostly forgotten the concept or shoved it aside completely. We have little foundational understanding of the very thing Jesus talked about more than any other when he walked this earth, and it's showing. It's showing in the blurred lines we've allowed between earthly kingdoms and God's kingdom. It's showing in how we date, marry, parent, age, and face death. It's showing in how we define ourselves and various "other" groups of people. It's showing in our individual pursuits at the expense of others, even within the confines of our churches. It's showing through what we're ambitious for and what we admire most. We're a confused people, saying we desire to live according to the kingdom of God, expressing a desire to participate in "kingdom work," but not understanding at all what it means to do so, aside from sprinkling Jesus in somewhere along the way.

The kingdom of God is ultimately about allegiance. Jesus described it as being like a seed, invisible to the eye, implanted and sprouting in the hearts of those who have pledged their lives to him.

And so, in order to understand and orient ourselves toward the kingdom of God, we must look at the heart. If our hearts are divided according to contradictory allegiances, we cannot and will not experience the joy and life Jesus promised us. Instead, we experience confusion, anxiety, isolation, and the painful consequences of the actions we take in allegiance to false kings.

We become grieved and starved.

So we will, in these pages, ask God to search our hearts, show us our allegiances, and restore what we've divided or kept from him.

We must first know that our hearts are *created* for allegiance. They are also designed to crave full satisfaction, and so we naturally give our allegiance to what we believe will meet our craving for that fullness—what we often call peace and joy. In other words, the form and function of our lives fall in line behind our heart's greatest allegiance. We act according to what we love and value most. We *give ourselves over* to what we love and value most.

For those of us who are in Christ, we've at some point come to the repentant realization that our heart is broken at its very core, because it came to us straight from Adam, factory-set on *self*, and therefore we are in and of ourselves irretrievably distorted in mind, body, and soul. If our own heart is our compass, we don't know what's good, beautiful, and worthy of our allegiance. We only know what our heart wants and follow where our heart takes us— and we've come to realize we've followed our own desires straight into the grave. We cannot make our heart beat, alive and healed. We cannot straighten our crooked desires. This recognition had us desperately seeking outside help, and God came. He offered our heart rescue from its sinful state through the life, death, and resurrection of his Son, Jesus Christ, and thus we were healed by falling in faith onto him. Our heart was made alive, and it awakened to knowledge of true worthiness: Jesus the King is worthy of *all* allegiance.

If you have not yet decided to give your life and heart to Jesus by faith, you certainly have already experienced a craving for more, for fullness and a sense of purpose and joy in life. The Bible says these things are found in surrendering yourself to Jesus Christ. He invites you to bring your broken heart—broken by your own sin—and to confess your need for his healing and rule. In doing so, he gives you his forgiveness and his rightness with God the Father. He promises to accept all who come to him, believing. And he promises to love you forever. He is worthy of your full allegiance, and you'll find a satisfying life in no one and nothing else.

At whatever point we come to Jesus, the seed of the kingdom of God is implanted in us, and our transformation to wholehearted-ness begins.

So does the war.

Because we remain in the body, while the *power* of sin is nulli-fied in our lives, the *pull* of sin remains. Every Christian continually forgets where life is found, what is true, and where this world is headed, so our battle is to keep our allegiance directed toward Christ alone. Our mind requires renewing (Rom. 12:2), our flesh picks fights against the Spirit (Gal. 5:17) working in us, and our heart is like dough with the gospel as its yeast—it must be kneaded and worked through every part.

We need to be aware that the war we're in is not a cultural war or a political war. The war we're in is a *kingdom* war, and the battles are happening every day in our mind and heart. Whether it's a mundane day or a moment of crisis, in whatever we face, we either set our heart's allegiance on who we are, what we want, and what we can do (or what we want others to do for us), or we set it on who God is, what God wants for us, and what he has done and can do. We choose to exalt and worship ourselves, or we choose the King and his kingdom. It's either a broken cistern that leaks water (Jer. 2:13) or a fountain of living waters that never runs dry (John 7:37–39).

This is the war we find ourselves in, and the prize is our allegiance.

When the Bible speaks about our flesh, it speaks not of our physi-cal skin but rather our orientation toward ourselves—to please ourselves and depend on ourselves. To speak of "the flesh" is to speak of *self*.

Self is a category holding a thousand beckoning options, and we each have our own pet self-focused allegiances we attempt to crown as king. Self as king makes life complicated and complex, because self as king makes demands and offers promises of glory but gives only misery and death. Self as king turns us in on ourselves, distorting truth, making each of us our own level, by which we hang everything according to our desires.

Some of us give our heart's allegiance to security. We believe money will give us that sense of security and alleviate our anxiety about the future, and so we orient our life around gaining and maintaining financial peace. We guide our children toward lucrative career options, and we believe the future is only as promising as the dollar amount in our retirement savings. We build a kingdom where money is king, not considering (or choosing not to believe) the instability and insecurity this king truly gives.

Some of us give our heart's allegiance to control. We have carefully crafted dreams and desired outcomes, both for ourselves and for those we love, and our deepest held belief is that we're completely capable of creating and molding our lives according to our self-made agenda. A rotating list of bestselling books are built upon this premise, promising we can be the lucky few who escape suffering or unexpected blows if we work hard enough. So we build a kingdom where "the good life" is king.

And some of you resonate with me. We are those who have a heart bowed down before the approval of others, willing to do whatever is needed to be knighted with belonging, acceptance, and love. We give our best energy toward building a kingdom where self-significance is king.

We're created for allegiance and formed as receptors ready to be filled up to full, but we so often gorge ourselves on what cannot actually fill us. If success and power are supreme, there is always more to grab. If image is of utmost importance, we must keep pace. If our appetite is king, we must have more, more, more. We go back again and again, trying to find a satisfying feast in tasteless rubbish. We beg the gift to be the Giver, a drop of water to be our ocean, the world to be our heaven. The Bible describes this pursuit as an attempt to grasp the wind (Eccles. 1:14). It's utter futility.

And yet we go back, again and again.

How do we find our way out of this cycle?

Bow Anew

As Kyle and I drove on the winding loop, and as I sobbed into my hands, I began to work backward, sifting through my emotions, following the trails of thought stemming from these emotions, and diving deep into the wells of my heart, asking above all that God would help me make sense of me. I felt bare before him, willing for the first time in months for him to thoroughly examine and test me.

We're often taught to be wary of our emotions, and I agree it's necessary to be wary of *expressing* our emotions however we want or *following* our emotions wherever they lead, but I do believe God's given us our emotions as signals that we need to examine further. In other words, emotions are often invitations to consider what is happening within our hearts, *specifically to whom or what we're bowing our hearts in allegiance.*

Tears may flow in lament and trust before God, but they also may flow because we desperately crave what we believe others are withholding from us that we think will fulfill us. We can know the difference when we consider whether or not we'd describe what we're experiencing as *life* or *death*.

This has become an important litmus test for me in reorienting my emotions around truth.

Am I sinking in feelings of condemnation, rivalry, frustration, shame, regret, hatred, or anger? These only stem from the roots of self-trust and self-glory, and the rotten fruit they produce is eventual death. This rotten fruit *feels* like death in us, because it is. If I examine what lurks beneath these types of feelings, I find a heart bowing toward self.

On the other hand, if I'm experiencing feelings of peace or hopefulness, as if my heart is settled despite the circumstances swirling around me, I am experiencing the full life that can only be given and cultivated in me by the Holy Spirit. These are fruits producing further fruit, and it feels like being fully alive, because it is. If I examine what lies beneath these types of feelings, I find a heart bowing in trust toward God.

My emotions that day on the winding road clearly showed rotten fruit.

In the preceding days, I'd been reading through the book of Matthew, my eyes landing constantly on Jesus's description of the kingdom of God, and I thought of it now in light of being grieved and starved. I thought about how, again and again, he contrasted two ways of life: either we live according to the kingdom of earth or we enter into the kingdom of God. *One is death, and the other life.*

The kingdom of earth and its many reigning false kings make promises they don't keep. It's not that they choose not to keep them; it's that they can't keep them. The kingdom of earth, reigned over by the lusts of the eyes and flesh, can only and always give death and decay.

The kingdom of God, however, promises life and gives it in ways that far surpass our hopes, desires, needs, and expectations.

One is death, and the other life.

This was how I knew I'd become confused again about the kingdom of God.

I was grieved and starved, because I'd been looking for life among orchards of death.

We tend to make the Christian life so complicated.

We make it about behaviors and spiritual disciplines and worldview and voting and social justice, and all of these are well and good in their proper place, but what the Christian life really comes down to is *allegiance*. In the daily grind of life or the difficult circumstances we face, do we bow to King Jesus or do we bow to self? In our singleness, our marriage, our vocation, or our parenting, do we bow to King Jesus or do we bow to self? In the privacy of our home or our work in the community, do we bow to King Jesus or do we bow to self?

There is only one King worthy of our heart's allegiance: Christ Jesus.

All other claims to the throne are bogus. They'll certainly promise, but they will not deliver. *There are no exceptions to this truth.*

So when we struggle to find peace or joy, when we feel restless or unsettled, when we succumb to the same old temptations, or when we seek escape or control, what we're really feeling are the effects of self-allegiance.

We prefer to label it something else, to keep things on the surface, at the level of behavior modification.

Most of us respond as I did when I was "weary" and "discouraged": we think we need new direction, that there is some answer out there waiting to be discovered. If we just knew what God wanted us to do, we'd move into the green pastures of God's peace. If we just got more organized or said the right yes and the right no at the right time, self-sufficiency would win us some measure of joy. If we were just a little better at self-control or self-discipline, we'd finally "arrive" spiritually and be done with these feelings of failure for good. If we just had the right relationships, we'd feel accepted and wanted.

Do you see where this sets our heart? On self. On standards and priorities set by self. On the agenda of self. On the desires of self. On the power and productivity of self, as if God is a bystander, looking on and hoping we get it right this time.

Self-allegiance is incredibly subtle and also incredibly dangerous, because it traps us in a cyclical pursuit where we are both the petitioner and the answer to our own prayers. We like to think outside influences are mostly to blame for our difficulties, but in reality self is *the* greatest threat to the life and peace we want for ourselves and others, because self asks us to double down when the foundation beneath us begins to crumble. And so often we do, not realizing our false allegiance.

Recently my husband and I were talking about our marriage. I asked him how I could be a better wife to him and to please tell me if I did anything that consistently annoyed him.

He said, "I don't like your relationship with Instagram. Occasionally you fall into these slumps after scrolling through and comparing yourself to other writers, and it really affects you. You talk to me about it, which is fine, but we're having the same conversation over and over again. Do you realize that?"

I hadn't realized that, and it was sort of painful to hear.

I had a choice then. I could quit Instagram forever and always. I could turn my smartphone in for a flip phone. I could vow to never compare myself with another writer again. These were my initial thoughts, because I'd much prefer to rearrange the symptoms than repent of systemic heart issues. Instead, because I'd been thinking so much about the kingdom of God, I thought about what this consistent behavior revealed about my heart. I sat in the discomfort of allowing God to examine my heart's allegiance. It was, of course, to myself and my own desires and glory. I wanted the opportunities *those* writers had. I wanted the numbers of people following me to tick up and up and up. I wanted a feeling of having reached the top, wherever the top was. *Broken cistern, give me a drink. Fill me to the full.*

I looked again at King Jesus, sovereign and good, acknowledged in prayer the ridiculousness of my obsession, repented of my self-allegiance, and bowed my heart to him once again.

This is kingdom work.

King Jesus

The simple act of bowing anew to King Jesus will change us in a thousand ways, and all those ways are avenues of coming more alive, the seed of the kingdom sprouting and bearing fruit in our lives.

Bowing anew is the ongoing work of the Christian in which we continually bring the previously hidden (to us) parts of our lives, freshly uncovered by the Holy Spirit, under the rule and reign of King Jesus.

Bowing anew is what this book is about.

We'll start with the King, because the kingdom of God is ultimately about the rule and reign of Jesus in every heart. We'll discover the kingdom he's building among those with bowed hearts—its culture, ways, and demands. We'll define kingdom work as joining with God to bring all things, including our own hearts, under the rule and reign of Christ. Because our hearts are set on "self," we cannot trust our natural inclinations and allegiances, so together we'll name these false allegiances in order to reject and resist them. We'll not only confess our broken-down allegiances and our inability to heal ourselves but also the lies we believe about God that fuel our misaligned worship.

My goal in writing isn't that we might, in shame, modify our behavior but rather to point out how we attempt to justify ourselves, prove ourselves, provide for ourselves, and secure ourselves apart from Christ. I'm going to call us out to a greater kingdom than what we can currently see—the kingdom of God is in fact here!—and to a greater King than any we might set up for ourselves.

As we begin to name our mute and impotent allegiances, we'll turn our gaze to Jesus, and find in him our heart's true King. He not only rules with all power, all authority, and all goodness but he's gone first in showing us how to live as embodied humans walking this earth with a heart submitted to the authority of God. He's told us who he is and what his kingdom is like, so we'll lean in to him in order to listen and obey.

Finally, under the leadership of the Holy Spirit, we'll rearrange and reorient in the ways necessary for our lives to reflect our allegiance to King Jesus. We'll do so, trusting that, as the wind and waves fell under Jesus's command, our craving for lesser allegiances will quiet and wither away, and over time he'll make us joyfully wholehearted.

We often live our days without thinking about why we do what we do and if these practices display allegiance to Jesus. Sometimes we focus on disciplines or behaviors instead of cutting to the root of what motivates and drives us. My goal is to guide you as you consider your heart first and foremost, allowing God to examine you and reveal himself to you in areas you prefer to keep hidden. When you worship rightly, you become aligned under the rule and reign of Jesus, you discover the blessedness of being his, and your desires to love and serve him grow. In other words, you will act according to your greatest love.

This is kingdom work.

Bowing to King Jesus may pain our flesh, but it rights our worship and heals our broken hearts with life, peace, and purpose.

Grieved and starved no more.

THE *hard work* OF *heart work*

1. What is your biggest concern or need right now?

2. What emotions is this concern or need stirring in you? What do these emotions indicate about where your allegiance lies?

3. How would you define *allegiance*?

4. If a friend shared this same concern or need with you, what would you suggest to him or her about what it would look like to bow to Jesus in this situation?

5. For further reading: Deuteronomy 30:15–20, John 6:25–40, John 10:10, and Galatians 5:19–25.

TWO

behold your king!

My philosophy in life is that anything can be made into a game. Most of the made-up games I play involve my husband, although he's rarely aware we're involved in such heated competition. Driving home from one location in separate cars? I'll sneak through the back streets in order to beat him home and encourage whichever child chose the winning car (mine) to cheer wildly when he pulls in behind me in the driveway. Painting a room? I'll get my side done faster. Folding laundry together? Watch me fly.

Efficiency, it seems, is the only game of life I can win anymore in these, my middle-aged years.

I used to have big dreams, like playing college softball or competitive tennis. In my wildest dreams, however, I would be a contestant on *Wheel of Fortune* or *The Price Is Right*—either would suffice—and not only would I be a contestant but I planned to charm the host while completely taking the bank. Identifying the phrase on the bonus round? Easy. Showcase Showdown? No problem. My sister and I played our own version of *The Price Is Right* so many times when we were kids that I'd practically trained as an Olympian in estimating prices of boats and bedroom suites.

One of my other favorite game shows when I was growing up was *To Tell the Truth*. My sister and I would sit side by side in the doorway between the dining room and the living room of our childhood home, eyes glued to the television. We weren't allowed to eat our popsicles in the living room, so we sat on the linoleum floor, leaned forward over the red carpet with our red popsicles, and watched reruns of *Gidget* and, of course, our beloved game shows.

On *To Tell the Truth*, before a panel of celebrities, three people were brought out of the shadows, each identifying themselves with the identical name and occupation. Two were imposters and one was telling the truth. The celebrities, most of whom were only celebrities because they rotated between various daytime game shows, would ask questions of the three in order to uncover who *really* was the person being identified by said name and said job title.

As a viewer, I judged according to the same stereotypes it seems the celebrities judged by: Could this woman be a construction foreman on a major job site in New York City? Would a professional rodeo clown look like *that*? How were their accents, voice inflections, or the details of what they said telltale signs of authenticity or of being an imposter?

Only one could lay claim to the unique name and specific role, and when the real person was asked to stand, we'd discover in the end whether we at home had guessed right or wrong.

My competitive self hates to admit that I was wrong much of the time.

Will the True King Please Stand Up?

If, as we've established, our hearts are designed for allegiance, then each person must make a dedicated search for who or what it is we're designed to worship. Who, in other words, is our true king?

I've already given away the answer in the previous chapter, but it's important we explore the question.

If we were celebrities on *To Tell the Truth*, sitting before a row of people claiming the throne, how would we decide who held true claim to kingship and which were imposters? Various people and beliefs in our lives may lay claim to the name King, but we'll know who is telling the truth based upon who can actually fulfill the job description.

So let's look at that job description, first by looking at the needs of the human heart and then by considering who could possibly rise to the challenge of meeting them. The heart is the inner person, what makes each of us who we are. Consider how, when a loved one dies, we view their body and say in grief, "That's not him," or, "That's not her." We say this because the inner person who once animated the physical body has gone.

First, in our humanity we can neither see nor touch the inner person. The king worthy of our heart's allegiance, then, must be able to see, know, and understand the inner workings of a person. He or she must have higher knowledge of and authority over the spiritual world than what we individually or collectively can possess.

Second, our heart comes to us broken by Adam's sin, and we further poison it with our own willful sin. The king worthy of our heart's worship must have power to mend our heart of sin's decaying effects, both Adam's and our own.

Third, our heart comes to us blinded to truth. Though we try, we're unable to find our way to the fountain of life. Lest you think we've at least found a sip of life on our own, consider how, if it were so, the progression of history would be moving toward a better world with less war and more cultural harmony. Like fools, however, we continually return to drink from broken cisterns, as we discovered in the previous chapter. Collectively, we turn toward political means or toward technological and medical advances. Individually, we turn toward sexual gratification, money and possessions, or volunteerism. We've found none of these have been a fountain of life. The king worthy of the heart's worship, then, must know the way to life and be willing to share it with those who seek his or her help.

Finally, we aren't hearts without a home. Our heart comes to us uniquely embodied in time, space, place, and skin. The king worthy of the heart's worship must also meet *every* heart's greatest needs no matter our generation, socioeconomic status, nationality, or education level. He or she must be above space and time, able to know and relate to the world as a whole but also capable of relating to each of us uniquely and personally.

As panelists, we've been given the title and job description, and now three contestants sit before us, claiming the kingship. Two are imposters; one is our heart's true king.

The first speaks. "The heart belongs to us collectively, and we engineer life according to what we consider good and bad. Our idea of good and bad changes according to our forward progress, but never fear, for under our rule we promise blessings of power, belonging, protection, achievement, and glory."

The second speaks. "The heart belongs to me, and so does life. I am enough to rule in this world, and I do rule. I'm capable of anything I set my mind to. I can figure out the way to life. I can tame the heart and its brokenness through hard work and discipline. I hold all power and authority. I can change circumstances through holding fast to a dream and to achieving that dream through sheer determination. Under my rule, I promise blessings of security, image, and comfort."

The third speaks. "I will question you, and you make it known to me. Where were you when I laid the foundation of the earth? Tell me, if you have understanding. Who determined its measurements— surely you know! Who has put wisdom in the inward parts or given understanding to the mind? Who then is he who can stand before me? Who has first given to me, that I should repay him? Whatever is under the whole heaven is mine" (Job 38:3–5, 36; 41:10–11).

We're on our faces, for this is no game at all.

Asking the true king to stand up has been a trick question, an analogy gone wrong. *Do you see why?* Because we've put ourselves as judge and jury of what's true, of how this world and our hearts work. This analogy reveals imposters, but it also shows how we often set our own parameters and standards of who deserves our heart's worship. We make ourselves determiners of our life in this world, determining kingship based upon what *we want to be true*, because we're innately bent inward toward self-preference and self-justification. In other words, we cannot trust ourselves to know where to give right allegiance. As Jeremiah 17:9 says, "The heart is deceitful above all things . . . who can understand it?" Contestant #1, the collective "us" of the human race and human culture, can't comprehend the heart. Nor can Contestant #2, the individual self.

Only God, the third speaker, can comprehend the heart and know our need, so our only response, if we truly want healing, truth, and life, is to see who he appoints as our heart's King.

The Crowned King

As God has ruled over all he's made, he has himself appointed the true King: his son, Jesus Christ, who walked the streets of Israel two millennia ago. Jesus seemed just a man to those who encountered him then, but he said such curious things that the mention of his name brought both adulation and accusation from vastly different groups of people.

He told the Roman governor, "My kingdom is not of this world" (John 18:36), who heard this as, "I am a king ruling a kingdom you can't see."

Jaws dropped in the synagogue when he read from the book of Isaiah, "The Spirit of the Lord is upon me, because he has anointed me" (Luke 4:18), and then rolled up the scroll and said, "Today this Scripture has been fulfilled in your hearing" (v. 21).

In the Old Testament Scriptures, those the listening congregation knew well, a man was only called "anointed" when he was chosen by God to be set apart for holy service unto God. The anointed were either priests or kings, men such as Samuel, Saul, and David, all who were tasked by God to lead God's people and speak God's words.

Jesus's Jewish hearers knew in that moment of silence in the synagogue that he was proclaiming himself God's priest and king.

They'd actually been waiting for this proclamation. God's promises strung backward like pearls on a string for centuries, each promise a juicy clue as to whom the anointed king would someday be. Jesus's listeners must have silently ticked through all they'd been taught about this promised one. God had promised the anointed would come through King David's lineage (2 Sam. 7:12–16). He would be human (Dan. 7:13) but he'd be holy, righteous, and powerful as only God is (Isa. 9:6–7). He would conquer sin and death (Gen. 3:15). His consecrated service to God would be to suffer in order to bring healing and blessing to all who come under his rule (Isa. 53). And this king would come proclaiming good news to those who desperately needed it (61:1).

In claiming God's anointing, Jesus announced the outline and intent of his kingdom.

At that point, however, these were merely words, spoken to a disbelieving crowd. After all, anyone could lay claim to the throne and demand their allegiance. What happened from that point on would prove or disprove that claim.

You may know the rest of the story, how Jesus called people's hearts to the surface and then addressed what he'd exposed with such grace and truth that people marveled, and how he healed physical infirmities in order to comfort but also as a show of authority over the physical and spiritual world. Finally, facing death, he was anointed with oil, not as the priest but as the priest's atoning sacrifice (Matt. 26:6–13). He did all that God said his chosen one would do, and because of his faithful service, God crowned him as King forever:

> He humbled himself by becoming obedient to the point of death, even death on a cross. Therefore God has highly exalted him and bestowed on him the name that is above every name, so that at the name of Jesus every knee should bow, in heaven and on earth and under the earth, and every tongue confess that Jesus Christ is Lord, to the glory of God the Father. (Phil. 2:8–11)

Jesus's death and resurrection were, in effect, his crowning ceremony,[1] for "from his cross, he has conquered kings."[2] At the empty grave, he was finally seen for who he is—the King of kings, worthy of every bowed knee and every heart's allegiance.

Including mine, and including yours.

Jesus is worthy of your heart's worship because he holds all wisdom, authority, and power in the spiritual realm and is therefore able to see, know, and understand the inner workings of who you are. His reign is forever, and he reigns in perfect justice: "Your throne, O God, is forever and ever, the scepter of uprightness is the scepter of your kingdom" (Heb. 1:8).

He sits high above all, but he looks low, willing to help those in the most desperate places: "For because he himself has suffered when tempted, he is able to help those who are being tempted" (2:18).

Jesus is worthy of your heart's worship because he conquered the power of sin and death and is therefore able to cleanse you of all your unrighteousness when you confess his name as Lord. He knows the pull of sin we face every day, and he offers us grace and mercy in the face of our sin. His throne, representing himself and his reign, is one of grace: "For we do not have a high priest who is unable to sympathize with our weaknesses, but one who in every respect has been tempted as we are, yet without sin. Let us then with confidence draw near to the throne of grace, that we may receive mercy and find grace to help in time of need" (4:15–16).

Jesus is worthy of your heart's worship because he is life and gives life abundantly to all who come to him by faith. He has the power to rescue anyone, and his time is spent interceding for those who are his: "He is able to save to the uttermost those who draw near to God through him, since he always lives to make intercession for them" (7:25).

Finally, no matter the time, space, place, or skin you inhabit, Jesus is worthy of your heart's worship because he is not limited to these things. He is King to all, yet he is also Lord to you.

Jesus fulfilled his service to God the Father, and we are the beneficiaries of his rule over every principality and power. He died in our place, offered his righteousness as healing and life to our hearts, and gives us his Spirit in order that we might actually obey God's first and greatest commandment to love him back with all of who we are. He lived with perfect allegiance toward God his Father so we might enjoy the riches of the kingdom with him.

Praise God! He's given us a King worthy of our wholehearted worship.

The King's Subjects

Today I am facing the same issues I've faced for months: a sense of loneliness, or maybe it's uncertainty over shifting life circumstances, or perhaps there are hurts I need to work through down deep in my core. Part of the problem, obviously, is that I don't know exactly what the issues are. I can't name them; I only feel them acutely, and these emotions are layered barnacles on the underside of my skin. When the alarm buzzes in the dark before the house creaks awake, I open my eyes and think first of what roils beneath all my calendar tasks me with for the day.

Yes, still there.

These thoughts are becoming as familiar as the dawn, and I keep asking myself what I should do about them.

This is my regular mode: attack, do, work, fix, create a step-by-step plan in order to work myself out of my emotional mess. These responses come naturally, and they are great qualities that enable me to lead and accomplish, but when it comes to matters of the heart, they are powerless and attempted in vain.

When I've opened my Bible in these recent days, every verse, every story, every passage has whispered, *Remember.*

Remember that you can't understand your heart.

Remember that you can't reach into your heart and change it. You can certainly alter behaviors and choose a different course of action, but the true work of sanctification happens only as you respond to the leadership of the Holy Spirit.

Remember that this is good news, because you have a King who can and, more importantly, *willingly* does. You are not expected to rule and regulate yourself. *Wait on him.*

I find peace as I locate myself once again in the kingdom of God, remembering that I'm safe under the rule and reign of King Jesus, rehearsing that he will help me.

This is why allegiance matters. It matters because we have a King who is all-good, all-powerful, and all-knowing, a King who cares for us and willingly takes responsibility to shepherd us. It matters because we're citizens of an unseen country and players in a larger story; we're not defined or confined by what is happening to us today.

But allegiance also matters because every single day we encounter claims for kingship that desire only to lead us into subjugation.

We're well aware of the claims from "out there" in the world, such as greed, hedonism, and sexual immorality. We're less likely, however, to consider the claims to the throne from "in here," whether in the modern church as a whole or inside of ourselves. Like my own current thoughts, these are more difficult to recognize and more difficult to name.

On *To Tell the Truth*, the imposters are believable because they take on the characteristics of the true person. The imposter we are most likely to believe as Christians is Contestant #2: self. Daily we experience thoughts, emotions, and desires that crown self as king, things like self-gratification, self-control, self-satisfaction, and comfort. Reliance on self and seeking glory for self sound really good, especially when baptized with Christian-sounding ideas. But we must understand that though self claims power and authority, we are impotent at best in matters of the heart. Self sidles in subtly, acting as though of little consequence, but it leads our lives astray in consequential ways. In self-authority, we're offered life but given death.

This is why we must consider our allegiances, not just once, when we give our lives to Christ, but rather every day and in every situation. The process of God making us wholehearted toward him—when our actions, thoughts, and desires align with the truth of who Christ is and what he's done for us—is ongoing. Wholehearted allegiance grows not as we seek to understand ourselves or take greater agency over our lives but rather as we seek to intimately know and love our King and put to death the decaying things that don't have a place in his kingdom.

Knowing King Jesus is the crux of the matter, because to know him is to love him, and to know how he relates to us is to know love. His is a love that drives out all fear, condemnation, pride, self-focus, and hatred—the very roots of death. In other words, he is life, and he brings life to those under his care. He makes us alive and fruitful.

Though at present we do not yet see everything in subjection to him (Heb. 2:8), he is now acting among humankind to relieve us from bondage to Satan.[3] The enemy's power is broken. He is bound. We're not bound to this earthly kingdom, this place of death and decay, any longer, because we have a King who made a way out for us.

Every generation and every person faces the question, Who gets to decide where my heart's allegiance goes and how I live? Will I seek my kingdom or his? Will I be subject to self or subject to King Jesus?

In the story line of the Bible, the kingdom of God shows us what's wrong and redefines what normal is for us. We live according to our own ways, which is actually living in abnormality, because this isn't the way God intended the universe to work. Normal is King Jesus, and his proclamation as King is that this broken-down world we see isn't the way it's supposed to be, and we don't have to live this way. He's currently forming the kingdom through the Spirit in the people who are in submission to him.[4]

The kingdom of God locates us in a story bigger than us and bigger than our generation. It corrects our tendency to bow to self as king and shows us how we only "find ourselves" as we pledge allegiance to Christ the King and take identity as his subject. As the only true King, he blows up all the things we build our lives on, which actually frees us from the disappointment and death that come from seeking any other false king. Because refusing to bow to self as king is the very moment when God's grace comes in.[5]

And grace is both rich and generous.

The earthly kingdom, with its many false kings, always requires our own effort and maintenance and is therefore defined by un-fulfilled promises. The kingdom of God, by contrast, is defined by grace. Grace doesn't merely remove our sin, although forgiveness is certainly an aspect of grace; grace adds as well. In other words, grace doesn't just gain us entrance into the kingdom but invites us to share in its riches.

As Christ the King slowly unbinds our grip on an earthly king-dom and binds us to a new one that is life and peace and security, we find God's kingdom is not *built* but rather *given* to us.

The kingdom of God can only be received.

THE  hard work OF heart work

1. In your life, how have you set your own parameters and standards of who deserves your heart's worship? What have those standards been?

2. Have you ever followed your own heart, thinking you know what's right or best, and then in the end realized that you'd followed your heart right into sin? Why is it important not to follow your own heart? What must we follow instead?

3. Go back through the chapter and list what you've learned about the nature, demeanor, and actions of King Jesus. Consider what it means that he is your King and this is how he relates to you. Does this knowledge require any reorientation in your thoughts or actions?

4. What does it mean for your life that your King sits on a throne of grace?

5. For further reading: Job 38–40 and Colossians 1:15–22.

THREE

receiving the kingdom of god

May 19, 2018, was a Saturday. I woke up before the sun, snuck out of the master bedroom, and tiptoed downstairs so as not to awaken a house filled with boys who cared infinitely more about sleep than joining me in what I was about to do.

I wanted quiet. Scratch that. I wanted quiet *and* coffee, so I could disappear half awake into what I knew would be a fleeting fairy-tale moment: Meghan and Harry's royal wedding.

The pragmatic side of myself tsk-tsked at my own frenzied excitement, knowing they are but humans who put their (pricey) pants on one leg at a time. But the girly side of me just wanted to see the dress, the groom's face when he saw his bride, the royal children waving to the crowd, and especially how this modern romance would play out before the world.

Snug beneath a throw, I opened my laptop, searching for coverage. With each breathless announcement of the bride's Rolls Royce proceeding closer and closer to Windsor Castle, I anticipated the moment Meghan stepped out of the car and into her new royal life. I wondered what she was thinking as her driver traced the route, as excited fans screamed her name and waved British flags back at her.

Could she ever have imagined, as a girl growing up in California, that she'd marry a British prince?

Perhaps that's why the world became intrigued and enthralled by Meghan. She was an American commoner, a divorcée (previously thought unsuitable for royal marriage), and an actress who'd once opened briefcases on *Deal or No Deal* upon Howie Mandel's command. Her unlikely coupling with Prince Harry proved to everyone watching on their laptops in America or in the streets of England that, somehow, unknown and unremarkable commoners can become claimants to a throne—or at least the *mother* to a claimant to a throne.

As I waited for her emergence from the car, I thought of how drastically Meghan's life was about to change. She'd once been unknown but now had become one of the most recognized and photographed women in the world. She'd once taken small roles on American soap operas, trying to make her way in the world, and now, because of whom she loved and who loved her, she'd be given the world.

A Kingdom Plunged into Darkness

There once lived a man who, because of who loved him, was also given the world. His name was Adam, and as the first man, he ruled as a servant-king in Eden alongside his queen, Eve. He cultivated the earth, named the animals, and walked with a heart bare and happy before God. The world in its fullness was his.

God himself had initiated this kingdom, where the people he loved would not only exercise wise dominion over creation but would be fruitful and multiply and enjoy abundant life beneath the protective umbrella of his good authority and provision. This is life as it was intended to be: God's people in God's place under God's rule and blessing.[1]

God's created world was one of a million yeses. To any request of Adam's for joy, peace, fulfilling work, and satisfaction in relationships, God smiled and nodded, delighted to give. In all those millions of yeses, there was only one no: Adam and Eve were not to eat of the tree of the knowledge of good and evil. In effect, this too was a yes to Adam's desire for abundant life; the no protected him from what he didn't (yet) know he needed protection from.

But in a world of a million yeses, Adam chose to pursue the one no. He and Eve together ate of the fruit.

Every time I retrace my steps to Eden, I cringe at their choice. I want desperately to enter into the narrative and plead with them, for those fateful bites have inked my own story. Their choice initiated a chain reaction of destruction, passing down through centuries and generations to me and to you.

In Romans 5:12–14, Paul equates this chain reaction to the spreading of death, similar to the spread of a contagious and fatal disease:

> Therefore, just as sin came into the world through one man, and death through sin, and so death spread to all men because all sinned . . . death reigned from Adam to Moses, even over those whose sinning was not like the transgression of Adam, who was a type of the one who was to come.

Sin entered the world through Adam, and with that, both physical and spiritual death came into existence. Paul personifies sin and death as though they are party crashers, interrupting a world of celebration and rejoicing, turning it into a tragedy and a funeral. They were trespassers entering into a situation where they weren't intended to be, and they came in through Adam's sin. The kingdom of God—*how life was meant to be*—seemed dismantled.

Though we weren't there in Eden, a part of us died in that moment with Adam. We no longer know what it means to be truly alive or to have a whole heart that beats for God alone. We can't imagine a world not in rebellion against God and against one another, or a world where all living things don't die. Instead we know alienation and separation, and we know death with such clarity that just the thought of it brings tears to our eyes. Every sad story flows like disease from Adam's decision.

What would we do to change this somehow?

We, of course, think we would have chosen differently than Adam did.

I prefer to think of myself as an individual, acting autonomously, who should be judged according to my own actions. The Bible, however, paints a picture of human solidarity. In Romans 5, Paul says it's like we were there with Adam, that we're as responsible as Adam, and that Adam's guilty verdict in the divine courtroom is ours as well. We have a representative before God, whom we did not choose but who acted for us, and we with him. Adam is our kingdom representative before God, and his DNA pumps fervently through each of our hearts.[2] To think we would have done better than him, we would have known better, or we could rule better is the very mindset of Adam, who attempted, in the name of "better," to usurp God's rule with a justified bite.

Adam's "better" was a prayer for his will to be done, for his kingdom to come.

And it did.

The kingdom of earth was born, and now every heart in every generation must find its way out of the utter darkness of being stillborn, buried six feet under. The darkness is the knowledge that we're not right with God, or at the very least we all at some level feel a sense of guilt, shame, or desire for more than who we are or what we have. Our earliest memories and every day since are entwined with the knowledge of good and evil, right and wrong, as well as our knowledge that try as we might, we cannot rid ourselves of the wrong.

We certainly try everything possible we know to drive the darkness away. We give our heart's allegiance away to political leaders who promise us national renewal. We throw the weight of change back on ourselves, believing if we only will do more and try harder, we'll bring light and life into the world. We lean on intellectualism, superstition, financial security, reputation, our children, job titles, or relationships in order to prove our rightness. Or we simply go with our heart where our flesh leads and with our flesh where our heart leads, assuming if we could satiate our desires we'd find ourselves most alive.

The only problem is that these pursuits may justify us in Adam's kingdom but they only confirm our curse in God's kingdom.

I've tried, as a perfectionistic religious girl, to drive out my darkness with goodness. "Watch me," I've said under my breath to the idea of imperfection. "I'll prove my goodness with goodness."[3] As if my very own heart could manufacture it through sheer determination. I imagine, as I consider my old ways, a seed beneath the soil sprouting up simply because I've wanted it to and thought of it in my mind. Magical thinking, this, imaginary and completely ineffective. The very fact that I cannot be perfectly good before a perfectly good God proves the darkness I'm in and confirms my curse.

The curse is earned, because the one who stands before the divine judge for me and for you is Adam.

Make no mistake, God still reigns. He reigned during Adam's coup. He reigned as death spread. He reigns today as sin and death continue their plague. Because he is holy and just, he reigns in judgment. He must punish sin or he would not be just in his decisions. As a result, when we're "in Adam," we're plunged into darkness in this kingdom of earth, and we don't enjoy God's blessings but rather a curse.[4]

The servant-king's crown has fallen off our heads, and we feel it every day.

A Benevolent King and His Kingdom

But remember! We have a King!

Scripture persists in telling its one narrative, beginning with Adam and Eve's exile from Eden, continuing with God's new creation of the Israelite nation, climaxing with the resurrection of Jesus and the birth of his church, and seeking the final consummation when all things will be physically seen at his feet. God is reclaiming his rightful rule and reestablishing the kingdom Adam and Eve plunged into darkness. As death spread through one man, now light and life are similarly spreading through the rule and reign of King Jesus.

What Paul is trying to tell us in Romans 5 is that we have options. If we don't like our representative who stands before the divine Judge, if we want to escape the curse of judgment Adam blanketed us all with, we can choose another ambassador to stand for us. If we don't want to continue living under the rule of a kingdom characterized by darkness, sin, and death, we can move and take up residence elsewhere, a place defined by light, favor, and life.

In other words, there is a place for us in the kingdom of God.

That's what Jesus came announcing when he began his earthly ministry. He said, "The kingdom of heaven is at hand" (Matt. 4:17), and what he meant was that he himself had come, within reach. As we discovered in the previous chapter, he is a King who shares himself with those looking to enter his kingdom. He didn't stay seated on a throne, high and lifted up, unaware of or unconcerned with the darkness spreading and destroying the lives of those he created and loved. He entered in, and his presence came like a blinding light, contrasting and therefore revealing the depth of darkness in our hearts. His holiness called our heart to the level of perfection, and just when our face fell downcast at our helplessness to meet such a demand, he met the demand for us. *The kingdom of God gives to us that which it demands.*[5]

Jesus talked about the kingdom of God more than he talked about anything else. He tried every which way to describe the unseeable, each description an invitation.

"The kingdom of God," he said, "is comprised of the meek, the hungry, the thirsty, the spiritually impoverished" (see Matt. 5:3–6). Well, that's just about any of us who've recognized the darkness of the world and who've felt the curse weighing heavy in our heart.

"The kingdom of God is like a seed," he said, "like leaven in bread" (see Matt. 13:31, 33). Something growing, something rising, something working. Something becoming wholly other than how it started.

"Are you tired and weary? Then come to me," he said (see Matt. 11:28).

In other words, there is a place for us in the kingdom of God, and this place is opened to us through Jesus.

This is why he talked about the kingdom of God so much: because he wanted to show people like you and me how we might enter and how we might have a new and perfect representative before God.

We enter by receiving.

God's kingdom doesn't demand we create righteousness in order to enter. He gives it to us. God's kingdom doesn't demand we create life in order to have it. He gives it. God's kingdom makes one demand: Repent! Turn! Decide! To repent is to receive the kingdom.[6]

Repentance sometimes seems like a harsh word, a weighty word, a fire-and-brimstone word, but when I think of repentance, I think of a child. As I'm writing, the window is open and I hear the laughter of a child as she tugs at her mother's hand. She's poised to run, but her mother's evident weariness slows the process.

Children rarely walk anywhere. They are persistent, insistent, and invariably trusting of their parents. They have everything done for them, and they know it without even considering it. Someone else will pay. Someone else will tell them the day's plans. Someone else will care for their needs. Someone else is in charge.

This is repentance: we enter the kingdom as a child, trusting in Someone Else's authority and provision. We don't pretend we can claw our way out of the darkness. We run to Jesus and stand with him in his light.

He is a King who shares, because he willingly stands before the divine Judge as our representative. He took the curse of God's wrath and judgment, reclaiming us from Adam and offering us the favor of God that he earned at the cross. Jesus is the source of God's blessing to us. What's his is now ours.

> The Father . . . has qualified you to share in the inheritance of the saints in light. He has delivered us from the domain of darkness and transferred us to the kingdom of his beloved Son, in whom we have redemption, the forgiveness of sins. (Col. 1:12–14)

What this means for you is that if you've acknowledged your sin (that you were born "in Adam") and your complete inability and powerlessness to raise yourself out of the death that's resulted, you can turn to Jesus and accept his offer to be your new representative. You are then "in Christ" and, through his work, have met the qualifications to enter the kingdom of God.

Judgment and the curse are removed, and now grace and mercy are yours to live in. You sit under the rule of King Jesus. That is to say, you are under his blessing.

You are either known by Adam and what he did or you're known by what Jesus did. God deals with us through a person; he sees us as that person is. If you are in Christ, his righteousness is your righteousness. His favor is your favor. What Jesus did, you did. You, because of him, have defeated sin and death.

Don't you see what this means, beloved of God? Doesn't your soul burst within you to think of it?

Because of who loves you, you're given the very kingdom of God!

The King's Kingdom

If we're no longer "in Adam" but rather "in Christ," we are, as Colossians 1 says, no longer residents of the kingdom of earth but residents of Christ's kingdom.

What does this mean exactly?

The kingdom of God is not something we often talk about, perhaps because it's intangible and mysterious in nature. We cannot trace its physical, political, racial, or religious boundaries as we would categorize nations or institutions or earthly kingdoms, so it's difficult to conceptualize.

What it means is that our feet are firmly planted on earth and we remain embodied people with flesh and blood, but our hearts have gone before our physical bodies into a new kingdom. Paul says it like this: "For you have died, and your life is hidden with Christ in God" (Col. 3:3). And like this: "But God, being rich in mercy . . . raised us up with him and seated us with him in the heavenly places in Christ Jesus" (Eph. 2:4, 6). We are not physically seated with Christ in the kingdom (yet), but we are spiritually seated with him, under his rule and blessing. What's his is ours.

And what's ours is his. We are his subjects.

The kingdom of God, then, is at its most basic level the rule and reign of Jesus Christ the King in the hearts of men and women who have subjected themselves to him, rejected the old kingdom and its ways, and sought and found a new home.

Every household, whether a married couple or roommates sharing a home, has certain ways of doing things. My husband, Kyle, and I have couple-friends who, every night, eat their dessert in bed, the husband typically choosing ice cream that he's microwaved down to liquid. Other couple-friends have a coffee maker next to their bed and enjoy a cup of coffee together in the morning before their feet touch the floor. A friend who lives with four other women gathers with her housemates for prayer every Tuesday morning at 7:45 a.m.

on the dot. In our home, our nightly routine is to head to bed at the same time and read side by side.

God's kingdom, similarly, is a household, a spiritual home (1 Pet. 2:5). We are God's people in God's place under God's rule and blessing.[7] We together are brothers and sisters, abiding with God our Father and Jesus Christ our Brother. And just as in any other household, there are ways we do things in our family.

In other words, the kingdom of God tells us who we are. We have a new citizenship, a new identity, because God has proclaimed who we are through Jesus the King.

We hear accusing whispers in our ears reminiscent of the old kingdom: *You are alone. You are unloved and unlovable. You are defined by your sin. It's up to you. You are hopeless. You'll never get it right.* These whispers seek to identify and accuse us, but they are, even more, lies about our God. They are meant to question his rule and reign, telling us that perhaps we aren't as secure and provided for as we thought we were.

We also hear siren songs calling from the old kingdom: *Happiness is available to anyone who would return and indulge. Success will satisfy. Your identity is really based upon who you're in relationship with or what you do for a living. Comfort is security, and security is comfort.*

But remember! We have a King! *And we have received his kingdom!*

When the British monarchy welcomes a new baby into the family, as William and Kate have done in recent years, an announcement is placed on an easel outside of Buckingham Palace. The announcement is a proclamation that something has changed and there is a new order in those entitled to the throne.

Jesus's life was itself a proclamation. Christianity is often considered merely a good idea as to how to live, but it is more than that. It is an announcement and a proclamation not of what we're to do but of what God has already done.[8] And what God has done is to take hold of us, pull us out of the darkness we've plunged into, and transfer us to light and life. What God has done is to proclaim our new identity.

This proclamation comes with a powerful combination of authority, action, and declaration: we are who he says we are. He has the authority to identify us. He has taken all required action to claim us as his. And he has made it clear how we receive the kingdom and come under his blessing.

The authority rests in the King's proclamation, and Jesus's hard-won proclamation of you is that you are alive, you are righteous, and you are identified as his beloved. You are secure in his love—nothing you can do or fail to do will ever change that. In a world of identity confusion, we are identified by our good King.

Because he has all authority, he also holds the right to rule in our heart. The kingdom of God is the rule and reign of Jesus in our heart, but it manifests itself in every area of our outward lives too: in our relationships, the way we spend our time, what we give ourselves to, and what we restrain or reject.

All Gain

Meghan gracefully appeared from her Rolls Royce to the sounds of cheers and fanfare, and I oohed and aahed aloud to myself over her wedding dress. I felt a twinge of sadness, however, as she took to the steps and I considered how her life was about to change. How does a duchess make new friends? How does she dart into Target for a new iron? Whom does she ask for marriage advice or talk with about the ins and outs of being a *duchess*? How does she get home to spend Christmas with her mom? Does a duchess attend her high school reunion or go for a walk alone in the sun?

She'd now be hidden behind the palace gates, behind the royal name. The crown, in fact, would hold sway even over her personhood. I felt sort of sorry for her, that after the fairy-tale wedding was over, she would lose everything she's known. But then I thought of how she now had access to anywhere the crown could take her: to jewels and riches, to heads of state, to seeing her chosen charities gain support. The world is her oyster because of who she is now, and it's all been given to her based upon who she's identified with.

We too lose everything as we enter God's kingdom, because acknowledging King Jesus means we can no longer pretend we sit on the throne. We lose everything worth losing, but we gain everything worth gaining. We have access to an imperishable inheritance because of Christ.

But most importantly, we have access to Christ himself. This is perhaps the greatest truth about your new kingdom life: you don't just give your heart to Jesus; *he also gives his heart to you.* He vows he will never remove his love from you, no matter what. He promises that not a single circumstance you've faced or will face can separate you from his love.

Pledging allegiance to God and walking in his ways is, in the end, a no-lose, all-gain life. How often do we count up only the costs, and lean away from others in self-protection, timidly fearful of what else God will require of us?

But hear these words. The desire of the righteous ends only in good. She gives freely yet grows all the richer. She gives away blessings and is herself enriched. She withholds nothing and is blessed. She seeks the good of others and finds favor. She who trusts in the Lord rather than in what she can possess flourishes like a green leaf. The fruit of a righteous life is a tree of life that also nourishes others (see Prov. 11:23–31).

I want to be that kind of woman. My first response upon reading those words was, "I commit to doing those things, because I want to be that kind of person." But I was immediately reminded that the kingdom of God is *received*, not built through my efforts. Heart always comes before feet and the righteous life begins with an allegiance to the King. When I embrace his rule rather than my own, I find myself hidden in him. He is my guard and protection.

He is my flourishing. As I trust in him, I can give myself away and find myself rooted and growing in true life.

Friends, as we hide behind him, we find that all is gain, because although we certainly lose ownership of ourselves and count the cost of rejecting an earthly kingdom for God's, the promise is that the loss always comes back to us through him as gain!

A life hidden in Christ is rich.

The generous life is rich.

A life focused on the good of others is rich.

A Godward life is, in the end, all gain.

There is simply no better place to be than under the rule and reign of King Jesus.

Why would we want anything else?

Because the war is real, and the battle is for our heart's allegiance.

THE *hard* *work* OF *heart* *work*

1. Are you in any way attempting to build a kingdom that glorifies yourself? If so, how? What fruits are you bearing from your efforts? Let this realization lead you to confession and repentance.

2. What does it mean to receive the kingdom of God as a child? What could that look like in your daily life?

3. What has it cost you to reject the kingdom of self and follow Christ? How has that loss been turned around through Christ as gain?

4. If everything Christ is and has is yours, then what is yours?

5. For further reading: Galatians 3:13–14, Romans 8:31–39, and Philippians 3:7–12.

FOUR

resisting the kingdom of self

This morning when the alarm went off, my first thoughts were as dark and gloomy as the predawn sky outside my bedroom window. *I don't want to get up. Just a few minutes more. How many hours until I can crawl back under these covers again?*

I considered the long task list crouching at my door: these very words I must think and produce, the hours I'll spend taxiing children to and from their activities, the food I'll make that'll be scarfed down by said children in five minutes or less at tonight's dinner table. I reminded myself of our appointment with the handyman, the laundry that required turning over from the washer to the dryer, and the text messages I needed to return in order to schedule more taxiing and more errands and more appointments.

Here in middle age, life is often routine and mundane. I heard about it before I got here from weary and worn pilgrims coming back around to tell me of the landscape ahead. Listening to their stories with my young adult ears, I couldn't imagine ever reaching the mountain's peak and then standing to look downhill at, God willing, what's left of my life. My days then were all about gain: gaining friends, credentials, credibility, a career, a husband and children, experiences, savings in the bank, knowledge, a house and all the things needed to fill and maintain it. I'd stored up, added on, and weaved my way through the possibilities with a happy, carefree clip in my step.

The pilgrims told me about what was to come, but I felt *for sure* I'd be the exception.

I've hit the crest of middle age and suddenly I see the loss coming—children are claiming their (beautiful) independence, parents are aging (beautifully), and more than that, the days are running together faster and faster. They are snowballing down the mountain, each one the same as the day before (wake, taxi, work, taxi, fall into bed). The gaining has become giving, releasing, letting go. There aren't many life-altering decisions left to make, as far as I can see. They've been made and now they play out, one by one, while I watch and experience the outcomes of my decisions.

And still, my desires remain. I'd like to do some things, go a few places, see the Lord in the land of the living. The list is extensive of what I hope to accomplish and gain. But I recognize now, perhaps for the first time, that I will go to the grave with unmet desires and unaccomplished dreams. I thought, in those days with that happy clip in my step, I'd eventually cross every finish line. I assumed the peak of the mountain was the end, as if life were a linear climb toward heaven.

Life is rather a jagged hike down toward dust. Not much that has been gained will remain in the end.

In this tension I feel, looking downhill, I wrap myself around whatever comfort and security I can find, clinging more tightly than ever, trying to squeeze life from dry bones.

I am not a very good Christian.

That was my first thought there in the early morning hours, and I opened my eyes and wondered at its merit, rehearsing it as if it were a truth I must memorize. I looked in the face of what crouched at the door of my heart, things I'd rather not think about, things I can't figure out or explain, things defying labels or over-the-counter cures.

I am in pain and have been for months, not a physical pain but rather an aching internal pain of hurt, a shifting in circumstances, and—what's most difficult to acknowledge—my own sin mixed and tangled in with it all. It's actually the hurt and the shifting that have *revealed* what lies within—the besetting sins, though long lying dormant, remain. I wouldn't have seen the truth without the pain, and now the question before me is how I'll respond.

I know clearly how I'd *like* to respond. I'd like to run away. Or I'd like to run at it, attacking, with a five-part plan meant to eradicate every painful twinge. But middle age and all the knowledge I've gained has evolved into a wisdom telling me this is a gaping hole that I, try as I might, am powerless to fill.

All I can do is wait, not for my circumstances to change but rather on God to change *me*. There is always hope, because I may not be a very good Christian, but God always holds and helps, and I trust he'll hold and help me through my doubts and wanderings.

Even before my toes touched the carpet, I was locked in my first fight of the day, wrestling to bring my thoughts, emotions, and desires in line with who my King declares me to be within the kingdom of God.

This Life Is a War

We learn our identity as being "in Christ," and it all sounds well and good and even straightforward, but when it comes down to the everyday stuff, the Christian life is not simple, nor is it straightforward.

We have often believed (and voiced) that becoming a Christian means life gets better or easier, but the Bible says this isn't true, that in fact we find ourselves caught in the middle of a war between the flesh we carry around every day and the Spirit who resides within us. The Spirit wages war against the flesh (Gal. 5:17) in order that we might know Christ and enjoy the fruits of righteousness, and the flesh fights back as if it's been mortally wounded.

Because it has.

When it comes to how our flesh fights, we can't discount the overt temptations of lust or greed or vengeful anger, and we're certainly not immune to these, but we want so desperately to discount the covert and more persistent and subtle temptations to exalt and depend on ourselves in our daily lives. This is perhaps the weapon most dangerous to our lives as kingdom citizens, because these temptations come masked with nice names like self-sufficiency and independence and a solid work ethic. Whether facing mundane days, holy yet unmet desires, or pain we can't escape, these are the exact occasions when the self sets itself up as king and promises what it can't fulfill: *salvation.*

I'm not talking about salvation as in whether or not we've been brought into the kingdom of God through Jesus.

I'm talking about salvation as in *rescue,* as in the rock on which we attempt to stand.

I'm talking about trust.

Will we say no to all other kings, including self, because we trust in God alone and the King he's set over us? Or will we concoct some mix of God and a safe, tangible plan B?

This is our fight on the daily: whether or not we'll hedge our bets, whether or not we'll cultivate wholeheartedness.

The Israelites warn us about this from their grave in the wilderness, that we might learn from their mistakes.

During the time when the prophet Samuel was growing old, the people worried about their future. Samuel had mediated for them well as both priest and prophet before God, but they needed a new leader, and by all appearances, humanly speaking, there were no options available. Samuel's sons, the next "sure thing" for the nation, didn't walk in the ways of God, so the elders looked around at how other nations were structured. They approached Samuel with their solution: "Now appoint for us a king to judge us like all the nations" (1 Sam. 8:5).

At first glance, this doesn't seem like such a bad request, but Scripture says it displeased Samuel and it also displeased God, because the elders hadn't thought to bring God into their calculations. Did they not already have a king? They had, in effect, spurned the perfect rule of the One who'd delivered, provided for, led, and protected them, and they'd turned toward another. They didn't *not* want God. They just wanted God plus a safe, tangible plan B like everyone else around them.

Samuel's response is a fair warning to us as well about plan B kings: *they will only take from you.* Samuel warns that a king appointed by people only takes sons and sends them to war, takes children and turns them into slave labor, takes daughters into his service, and takes crops in order to feed his servants (vv. 10–17). Samuel knew what less-than kings do: they take our best and then make us their slaves.

Samuel tells the Israelites what the end of it all will be: "And in that day you will cry out because of your king, whom you have chosen for yourselves, but the LORD will not answer you in that day" (v. 18). The Lord would not answer, because they'd asked their desires of a king who could not fulfill them.

We tend to believe the same as the Israelite elders: What will it hurt to have God and also hedge our bets a little? Rather than grieving and lamenting difficult experiences before God, we kick our negative emotions down the road a ways through shopping. Rather than casting our cares upon Jesus, giving him our weight to carry, we worry and fret and calculate. Rather than obeying the King's command to live at peace with others, we secretly harbor resentment and unforgiveness. Rather than trusting God has wiped away our every sin, we swirl in constant activity, a sort of penance through good works.

We want to believe we can pledge allegiance to King Jesus and also throw our heart to human kings or human things. But the Bible is plain: one cannot love both God and riches (Matt. 6:24). A divided kingdom cannot stand (12:25). Jesus is our King, not merely a wise consultant we turn to when we need to know what to do. And anyway, a divided heart is actually not divided at all: it's chosen sides, and as evidenced by the Israelite elders, a divided heart is one that's spurned God.

We turn toward false kings who we think will give us comfort, security, belonging, approval, validation, love, sexual gratification—but in the end they only take.

They promise life but give death, the opposite of what King Jesus does.

Author David Foster Wallace, who as a seeker dabbled in religion and religious thought, aptly describes the death we experience under the rule of false kings:

> [In] the day-to-day trenches of adult life, there is actually no such thing as atheism. There is no such thing as not worshipping. Everybody worships. The only choice we get is what to worship. And the compelling reason for maybe choosing some sort of god or spiritual-type thing to worship . . . is that pretty much anything else you worship will eat you alive. If you worship money and things, if they are where you tap real meaning in life, then you will never have enough, never feel you have enough. . . . Worship your body and beauty and sexual allure and you will always feel ugly. . . . Worship power, you will end up feeling weak and afraid, and you will need ever more power over others to numb you to your own fear. Worship your intellect, being seen as smart, you will end up feeling stupid, a fraud, always on the verge of being found out.[1]

This is what we must remember in the face of our daily fight: even the "safe" plan B kings are deadly. Bowing even slightly to anything or anyone but King Jesus will quickly turn to insatiable desire, and wicked desire leads to wastelands. All other kings promise what they can't give, including the king of self.

We, like the Israelites, receive what we ask of our kings. From kings who rule in this earthly kingdom, we receive slavery and spiritual death. But from King Jesus, we need only ask, only run for refuge beneath his rule, and we receive.

The Battle of Tuesday (and Every Day)

The trouble is that we don't often understand what it looks like for Jesus to be King on a Tuesday in March when we're late for work and irritated about something, though what exactly we don't know. We recognize we need Jesus as King on the cross, because we know our hearts are as dark as they come, and we're in desperate need of forgiveness and restoration. But in the day-to-day, we struggle to appropriate faith and remain wholehearted before our true King.

So how do we recognize and resist our plan B kings? How do we live in allegiance to King Jesus alone?

First, we look for signs of death.

Take, for example, my own bout with futility before my eyes even opened this morning. The feeling of despair, of wanting to run away or attack with my best efforts—these are signals, remember, of something producing death in me. If we feel a sense of death or condemnation or something being *off*, it's often a sign pointing toward misapplied allegiance. I don't think, of course, that every emotion speaks truth or that every wave of despair is solely spiritual and not sometimes physiological. But if a pattern has developed, if there is a nagging stench of death—and for me, this has been exactly the case—then I must inspect where my heart bows. What idol am I protecting? What king am I requesting God give me aside from him? What promise do I believe this faux king will fulfill if I bring it my allegiance?

These are important questions every Christian must have in their battle arsenal.

I myself have been prayerfully asking these questions for months on end. Uncovering the root of temptation or sinful allegiance can at times be an extensive process that God takes us through. We cannot diagnose our heart as we would a broken bone beneath an x-ray machine. We can only bring our heart to God and plead, "Search me, O God, and know my heart! Try me and know my thoughts! And see if there be any grievous way in me, and lead me in the way everlasting!" (Ps. 139:23–24). In other words, we wait for God to diagnose what we ourselves can't possibly see. Sometimes he responds immediately through his Word, but most of the time he lets us hang on his silence, because the silence often reveals even more in our heart he's preparing to address in his perfect timing and with his perfect healing.

This silence is, however, when temptation sets in, and when we're most prone to run into the arms of our preferred false kings. Our thoughts and emotions only clang around louder inside in the waiting, and in order to resist false kings, we must learn to sit within this tension.

My own thoughts in these months have been insistent.

Figure out what to do.

Figure out what needs to be fixed and fix it.

It's up to you to reconfigure the relationships that feel off.

It's no use; the situation is hopeless.

You are hopeless.

Sometimes I have succumbed to these temptations, fending off my own true responsibility, fueling my bitterness with self-righteousness. Other times, I have simply cried and whispered under my breath, "Oh, Lord, please help me."

It's taken many months of fits and starts, and many months of begging God for help and release from the sadness and the flares of emotion and bitterness. I've had hints of what was to eventually be revealed: a sermon that struck something in me on bringing other people in through confession of sin, an interview on my podcast with a woman who described a relationship broken apart, an understanding of some sort of throbbing obsession inside of me.[2] Each time, I felt the Spirit nudging me to pay attention.

Finally, *finally*, seemingly out of nowhere, the thought struck me as so right and so unignorable: *envy*. My prolonged malaise, like a low-hanging fog, had been an envy of the belonging others seem to be experiencing while I felt left out. What I'd been experiencing was my own sin of envy, and I knew I needed to confess it immediately, both to God and to the one most affected by it.

But it wasn't merely the envy God pointed toward with conviction and hope. It was also what my flailing about in those many months had revealed: I'd looked for peace, an end to the war raging, in a plan B king. I'd looked mostly to myself and my own wisdom to rectify the situation. I'd chosen to blame and resent others, full of self-righteousness. Most significantly, I realized that in a year when my circumstances and roles had shifted beneath me, I'd clung to relationships as my savior. When those seemed to be shifting as well, my fear turned to a demanding, entitled, fragile desire. I flung that desire before people, waiting for them to give and finding only disappointment when they didn't give enough. Because no one can give what God alone can.

Sit in the Tension of Change

When we find signs of death, we must then turn and seek life.

I went to the one most affected by my envy and told her about it, as if she didn't already have a vague knowledge that something weird had come between us. Our sin never affects just us, does it? We like to think it's inconsequential, but without fail it ripples outward, hurting those closest to us and distorting our relationships.

Our false allegiances have consequences.

Even before she and I met up for coffee, I felt great relief. In confessing my sin to God, a light shone into my dark and cavernous parts, clearing away decay and replacing it with his forgiveness and hope. My outlook on my relationships—not to mention the entire previous six months—shifted, and I understood how God's gracious hand had been guiding me through all along. He'd known everything in my heart the whole time, but he was revealing it to me slowly, in pieces, so I wouldn't be crushed. How patient and careful he is. How good.

I took my lightness into our coffee, finally able to release the self-protection I'd worn around my friend like a warrior's shield for far too long.

She was gracious, of course. She'd been patient, waiting me out, waiting for me to come back around, ready as always with her friendship.

Upon our goodbyes, I got in my car and sat there feeling the sun pour in through the window across my arm but also feeling so much more. I considered how good, how life giving, it is when my heart is properly aligned. Joy is facing the right direction after so much confusion. There was something of life bursting in me, the life promised by King Jesus when we bow in allegiance to him alone. He was giving to me according to his promises.

But then a weight entered. I'd seen my own allegiance to belonging rise above all other allegiances, a good desire for relationship twisted sideways. I'd confessed it to God and others, but confession is not and would not be enough. Now I'd have to make good on my confession and actually *change*.

And changing is the hardest part.

Recognizing our false king is only the first step. Then we need to change. Again, we must be careful we do not turn toward self as ruler and master at this point.

We're so set on changing ourselves as the peace to end our internal war, but can we actually change our hearts?

And yet we need change. We need rescue in our constant fight with temptation to return to earthly kings. We need help to live according to the kingdom identity we've received.

Thankfully, although we can't change our hearts, there is something we can change. We can change to whom we bow, because our right allegiance determines our right actions and behaviors. John 14:23 says it like this: "If anyone loves me, he will keep my word." Love comes first.

Heart comes before feet; where the heart goes, the feet will follow. If we love King Jesus, we bow our lives to King Jesus and align ourselves to his kingdom ways, for we long to please those we love.

Do you see how I tried to turn toward myself or toward others to right what felt wrong in me? This is an allegiance that takes me away from King Jesus and causes me to act in ways that inevitably harm me and my relationships with others.

Do you see how much trusting in God often means waiting on him to move, act, and reveal rather than turning to our own religious deeds, plans, escapes, or fixes? This is what it means to crucify the flesh, and this is *hard* stuff, primarily because temptation pulls us toward setting up a king we can see and touch and hear, as the Israelites did, when we already have a perfect one. In the waiting and the stillness of God, temptation tells us lies about his goodness, provision, rule, and leadership. Know this: the Christian life is one of misery and despair if we don't believe we have a King who gives, not just for our rescue from eternal separation from God but for our everyday Tuesdays when we sit beneath a cloud of confusion, insecurity, or temptation.

When we know we have a King who gives, we fight sin and the flesh, not by turning to false kings but by turning and seeking first the kingdom of God.

Seek First the Kingdom

How do you think about spiritual transformation? Does your mind immediately go to some sort of mental checklist? Do you think of specific actions you need to take? Do you feel hopeless that you can change in certain areas of your life that have plagued you since forever? Do you hold someone else as your standard and try to imitate them?

Just how *do* we change and grow when it's matters of the heart we're talking about?

We seek first the kingdom of God.

I heard Matthew 6:33 quoted a million times growing up in the church: "But seek first the kingdom of God and his righteousness, and all these things will be added to you." I never understood what the actual kingdom of God was, nor how to seek it. And what does it mean that "all these things will be added to you"?

Each time I heard or came across this verse in my teenage years, in my immature, performance-driven mind, I immediately pictured an illustration I'd seen from my Sunday school teacher in which she'd presented one large marble, a handful of smaller marbles, and a jar with a lid. We teenagers were tasked with fitting all the marbles in the jar, starting with the smaller marbles and then the large marble. Of course, we couldn't do it; the large marble on top prevented the lid from closing. Then we were asked to reverse the order, placing the large marble in first and then the smaller marbles second, at which point we discovered that the lid closed and, therefore, that Jesus should always come first in our daily priorities. We should seek first the kingdom and then everything else would fall nicely into place. I took that to mean that if I started my mornings off with a good thirty-minute "quiet time," the rest of my day would go swimmingly, evil spirits having been properly warded off. *I'll scratch your back, Jesus, if you scratch mine and give me everything I want and nothing I don't.*

Another favorite guilt-trip question was about spiritual disciplines: "Did you spend more time adorning your outward appearance than you did with Jesus?" I always thought of how much time I spent blow-drying, curling, and spraying my hair and could only hang my head in shame. I just knew I was a horrible Christian.

These are the illustrations and questions I associated with seeking first the kingdom, ingraining in me that God's kingdom is all about my behaviors and whether or not I clocked in more time in prayer than in hair. It was as if I held the levers for God's blessing and action—and there were lots of levers, and I had better get it exactly right, boy howdy.

I think too many of us live this way, believing that Christianity is about what we do and about getting the religious to-do list finished before we get to heaven. Trouble is, we're being fed more and more to-dos. If we take our notion of Christianity from social media, journalism, music, blogs, books, or the neighbor down the street, we can easily get confused—what really matters? What is being a Christian really about?

It likely would have been easier if Jesus had given us a checklist to follow, but he simply said, "Seek first the kingdom." He said this as he compared religious behavior that appeared right on the outside with the internal reality of "rightness" according to God. In other words, he addressed the heart. He mostly poked at the Pharisees, who went through their rituals for show and in order that they might validate themselves to themselves. God was, according to Jesus, far removed from this circus.

He also contrasted his kingdom with the ways of the nonreligious, who react to the daily concerns of life with control, anxiety, worry, and striving to get, gain, and maintain.

A heart focused on self can build a religious kingdom on good behavior or an earthly kingdom on want, but his way, Jesus said, is different entirely. Those who seek the kingdom of God simply seek Jesus as King, and cast all of who they are on his action: his rule, his protection, his direction.

What he's saying to those of us who're listening is that our hearts and minds are not to be divided. Seeking first the kingdom is synonymous with, "Love the Lord your God with all your heart" (Matt. 22:37). We have one job, one focus, one action, one identity, one priority: to gladly seek the rule and reign of Jesus over every part of our hearts and lives. We put all into and on King Jesus. He is our one allegiance. We're not called to multiple allegiances, nor a checklist of right things to do. His rule will play out in a thousand ways, but those thousand ways are up to him to decide and direct. Our task is to seek his rule over us and obey his commands.

So for the single, the goal is not marriage. For the married, the goal is not the perfect marriage. Whether working at a cubicle in Chicago or gathering crops in Ethiopia, whether an invalid with a chronic illness or a student on the cusp of college, whether a vocational pastor or an addict broken down in rehab, the Christian's focus is undivided allegiance. We place ourselves at the feet of Jesus and echo his submission to the Father: "Not my will, but yours, be done" (Luke 22:42). This aligns us with the Creator of the universe and keeps us in the path of life.

Seeking first the kingdom, then, is remembering we have a King and living accordingly.

The Pharisees refused the King, and the gentiles didn't know the good and gracious King, but we do know. We know all the reasons we have to be secure and content under his rule.

We know we're not left to our own devices, as those are who seek a religious or an earthly kingdom. When Jesus says, "Seek first the kingdom of God and his righteousness, and all these things will be added to you," he is telling us to seek his rule and reign by coming under his righteousness by faith, bringing anything that troubles us or concerns us under his care, and then watching for how God provides, because he will. We send every thought, every choice, and every trial through the filter of the kingdom story.

So how do you change? You seek first the rule and reign of Jesus.

Out of the overflow of a properly aligned heart, the mouth speaks and the obedience follows.

Soon, instead of signs of death, there will be signs of life everywhere.

Look at King Jesus

When I sat in the car after confessing envy to my friend, I recognized how my heart's desire for belonging was actually a hunger. I longed for filling, for satiation, and I'd been wantonly giving my allegiance and attentiveness to the people, opportunities, and things I believed would provide it for me. I'd also vacillated between avoiding and obsessing over what prodded at my idolatrous desire.

I know what hunger looks like. I have two teenage boys and another coming up in age behind them, and every night, not even thirty minutes after dinner, they come back to the kitchen, ravenous for more. I feed them what I think are filling, protein-enriched foods, but still, some nights they return for entire second or even third meals. I am at the grocery store almost daily, stocking up again and again and again.

Our hearts too are constantly hungry, whether for love or acceptance or success or relief from trouble. And we go where we think we'll find fullness, sometimes without even thinking about it, and mostly to acceptable idols like volunteering or caring for others in return for love and validation. Most of the time we don't even recognize our hearts are hungry. We, like I did, just feel off-kilter and uncertain, and we grab at what makes us feel most stable.

For us to seek first the kingdom, however, means that we seek our hunger's fulfillment in King Jesus every single time and in every situation. Every growl and grumble signaling our hunger sends us running to our King.

When we run to our King, we look and see again whom we've sought refuge under. This is our true stability.

I think of Numbers 21 as our example. In this passage, Moses and the Israelites were in an in-between place, no longer in Egypt but not yet in view of the Promised Land, and in their instability and wobbly fear, "they became impatient" and reached for the crutch of complaining. They complained against God and Moses both. Paul actually uses this story in 1 Corinthians to warn his readers against idolatry as a response to desire and temptation. Instead of running to God and remembering his provision for them, the Israelites' complaining was evidence that their hearts had run away from him, seeking refuge in some other option.

God disciplined them by sending poisonous snakes, and the people quickly saw their error. (I would too if a bunch of snakes were at my feet.) Moses prayed for the people and the Lord gave, in response, a physical and tangible picture of his forgiveness: "Make a fiery serpent and set it on a pole, and everyone who is bitten, when he sees it, shall live" (Num. 21:8).

Seeking first the kingdom looks much like this. We are wrapped in flesh and bitten by sin. God gave us a King who was like us, wrapped in flesh and aware of all our hungers, but who didn't succumb to sin. He hung on a pole in our place so that any time we feel the pang of hunger or the bite of sin, we go again and look at who he is and what he's done for us.

There, at the cross, we find once again everything we've needed and will need. We remember we have a King and that we're in a kingdom.

Our hearts truly find their satiation in him.

What I'm speaking of in this entire chapter is the practice of repentance. Seeking the kingdom and repentance go hand in hand. We enter the kingdom through repentance by faith. And we seek the rule and reign of Jesus through repentance when his Spirit points out the false kings we've run toward. Repentance unites us with Christ, and repentance continues us on toward Christlikeness. We build our lives as Christians upon repentance—a constant awakening to where we are, where exactly our hearts have gone running away toward false kings, and running back to gaze at Jesus. Change, in other words, is a long process, and it's fueled by repentance.

As Christian ethicist Russell Moore says,

> It's true that [repentance doesn't] stop your stomach from grumbling. You want what you want. But the discipline of God teaches you, slowly, to put old appetites to death and to whet new ones. Through

the Spirit of Christ you learn to crucify "the flesh with its passions and desires" (Gal. 5:24). That's hard. It usually means hunger or economic want or sexual frustration or familial longing. But through it we learn to see that life is about more than acquisition—whether acquisition of possessions or orgasms or pleasant memories. The temporary hunger can cause us, with our Lord Jesus in the wilderness temptations, to turn away from momentary satisfaction . . . and toward more permanent things.[3]

More permanent things. That is the kingdom of God: permanent, unshakeable, not yet seen but our very real future.

And so, each day, and in each situation, and even when we don't exactly know what's happening in our hearts, we pray the prayer of repentance, the one Jesus himself taught us: "Thy kingdom come, thy will be done." This is a prayer that leads us away from self-rule and self-agenda and the millions of allegiances whispering from the starving desert. This is the prayer that returns us under the rule and reign of Jesus. Repentance is aligning ourselves with our true identity, of relaxing into his possession of us and knowing it's where our greatest joy is found. We seek him, and all he is becomes added to us.

This is what Jesus means when he says, "and all these things will be added to you" (Matt. 6:33). When we seek refuge under the rule and reign of Jesus, we receive all he has to offer. He adds to us what we're lacking, leading us with his forgiveness, provision, grace, peace, knowledge, and wisdom.

Repentance, though painful at times, is a gift in the kingdom of God. Because through repentance we find life.

The Culture of the Kingdom

As we seek first the kingdom, and as we're added to by the King himself, we soon find that Jesus sends us out into the world with new ways and rhythms. We live differently than others do—more purposefully, more confidently, and more hopeful toward the future. Our allegiance *always* reveals itself.

The good news is that Jesus taught us how to live as a citizen in his kingdom under his rule. He's pointed to the path of life, so we don't have to guess or blindly feel our way. He's told us how we'll know if our allegiance is truly to him and him alone, and he's challenged us to let go of false kings.

So together, in the next section of this book, let's go to King Jesus and listen to his words, that we might align ourselves with him and the ways of his kingdom. He'll help us recognize our natural temptations, our plan B kings, and he'll dismantle them one by one. He'll show us how he and his kingdom are better and more worthy of our allegiance. Finally, he'll teach us how to live according to kingdom ways and our kingdom identity, and we'll explore daily practices that invite his Spirit's help in order to do this.

Just as we each have a unique personality, we each have individual tendencies toward specific allegiances other than Christ. I've already shared some of mine with you: escape, control, self-sufficiency, and a desire for belonging leading to envy. As we move into the next section of the book, ask the Lord to show you your own tendencies and how these allegiances are not fulfilling what they seem to promise. These allegiances are telling you lies about God and keeping you from a full life, so it's important to name them and call out their lies.

As we go, we must remember that we've been given the gift of repentance. We can run back to Jesus and gaze upon his mercy and grace, and we can experience restoration and wholeness over time, by his grace, and begin to "bear fruit in keeping with repentance" (3:8).

As we go, we'll find that the culture of the kingdom is life, and it's ours for the taking.

THE *hard work* OF *heart work*

1. The Israelites didn't *not* want God. They just wanted God plus a safe plan B king like everyone else around them. How do you resonate with the Israelites?

2. What are your plan B kings? To help uncover your false kings, consider these questions: What are you most anxious about? What are you living for? What are you working for? What do you boast in or place your confidence in? What, if you lost, would make you wonder if you'd be okay?

3. Can your plan B kings withstand the full weight of your hope? Why or why not?

4. What signs of death do you see as you've pledged allegiance to these kings? In other words, what are these false kings giving you in return?

5. How is repentance a gift for you?

6. What will it look like in your daily life to seek first the kingdom of God? What sort of necessary tension will this create for you?

7. For further reading: Numbers 21:4–9 and 1 Samuel 8.

PART TWO

false

kings

FIVE

anxiety

I saw him in an unexpected place at an unexpected time, and as we sat down for a moment to talk, he could not look me in the eye. This precious one, my brother in the faith, seemed to be elsewhere. He appeared weary, and I wanted not only to call him back to our conversation but to call him back to himself.

I probed deeply, as I tend to do, asking pointed questions I hoped were empathetic and understanding in tone, and he answered openly, sharing how anxiety had come to grip his mind and, soon afterward, his body. He was fighting back, he had good support, and he wanted me to know what he'd discovered about himself and about God.

So I listened, and as soon as he walked away, I scribbled down everything he said on the nearest piece of scrap paper. I wanted to remember his hard-won wisdom. I wanted to sink it deep into my own mind, a mind that felt as if it were a pie sliced into tiny slivers, each meant for something and someone else's consumption. I wanted to gather up those slivers and piece them back into wholeness beneath the hard-won truths my brother had shared with me. I wanted to remember what he'd said, because anxiety is a constant temptation for me.[1]

Truthfully, it's never far from any of us, forever lurking in the shadows, coaxing us to give it our undivided attention.

Anxiety is, after all, a temptation of attentiveness, *consuming* attentiveness. Anxiety seeks to fill our minds with thoughts and emotions that do not allow us the space or energy to focus on what *is* actually worthy of our mind's attention and heart's affection, which is why *attentiveness* is another word for *allegiance*. Anxiety is a false king that demands our constant attention, and therefore our heart's undivided allegiance.

What would this king turn our attention toward? What would it have our mind consumed by?

Anxiety is the "distress or uneasiness of mind caused by fear of danger or misfortune,"[2] so this king demands allegiance to a fear of the future. King Anxiety, on repeat, asks, "What if?" and "How are you going to do this?" and then points to all the circumstantial evidence for uncertainty and hopelessness. The answer to self is always self, which we feel as an unstable path into the future. Because it is.

Anxiety is at epidemic levels, especially among our younger generations, who've been glued to technology and social media since they can remember. This combination of technology and anxiety is no coincidence. Social media pulls us out of our present mind and localized body and sets our attention on global events and needs but rarely offers us any meaningful response. Very real events have become almost entertainment-like, people we faux-know through our phones are only able to be consumed, criticized, or of service to us, and we've begun to believe that we're not only capable of being everywhere at once but that we *should* be everywhere at once, as rechargeable as our phone batteries. We also see what the possibilities are through the lens of other lives: how we *could* be parenting or what *should* be financially possible at our age. We don't know how to discern between possibility and localized faithfulness, and we simply don't know where to mentally attend anymore, because we're everywhere at once, and we feel the pressure of being all there, knowing all the things, and doing it all perfectly.

We often feel anxiety rising in our heart, because we've trained our brain to think and attend separately from the body we live in, a body that is limited by design. Anxiety draws us out of our body and out of today—the day we can see and touch and experience— and sets our mind on a future we can't see or touch or know. We give attention, in our anxiety, to a million rabbit trails that are asking a million questions of us. *What if this happens? What if that doesn't happen? How can I prevent this from happening? How will I do that? How can I make sure this happens?* We make contingency plans for potential future scenarios that may or may not actually come true.

Whether driven by fear, performance, or ambition, anxiety is so prevalent in our Western culture that it's become an allegiance we believe is normal and harmless. The trouble is that anxiety is a false king who will ask for a little attention and then turn around and consume us fully. If we follow one little trail of worry as if beside a bubbling creek, anxiety soon opens like a dam upon us, and we're suddenly overcome and disoriented. We can't then find our way back to the path we deviated from on the trail, the starting point for this whole mess.

But I can tell you the starting point for our mess: it starts with lies, both about ourselves and about God. Humanity is driven by a quest for godlike supernatural capacity, and this is the lie published in plain English: we strive for omniscience and omnipresence. The lie at the root of our anxious rabbit trails is that this achievement is possible, that we can sit as an equal with God, who is all-knowing and everywhere at once. The lie of anxiety is that God is not capable of all-presence but we ourselves are; that God won't provide but we can provide for ourselves. Anxiety feels like the pressure it is because we willfully attempt to take on the weight and responsibility of being God. Anxiety is, as most of our false kings are, an allegiance to self.

Do you tend to bow before King Anxiety, believing that fretting, worrying, and thinking through every possible contingency is going to eventually give you the peace and security you bow to it for? Are you anxious that you don't have enough, you aren't as good as someone else, or that you'll lose what you already have?

I want you to picture anxiety in your mind as an actual wooden statue sitting in a prevalent place in your home. How much of your day are you spending at the feet of this king? How much does it get of your time, energy, and best resources? How is it limiting your love and faithfulness to the one true King?

And now consider these questions: Is this king worth living for? Working for? Placing your confidence in? Is this king giving you what you seek—total security? I don't know you but I know myself, so I already know the answers to these questions.

We're all prone to borrowing grief for ourselves from the future in the form of anxiety.

An Engaged Father

Fear has filled my life in the past few months. About a month ago, God showed me the source of this fear. It was coming from the idea that my fruitfulness is up to me. I'd buried myself in activity, hustling in order to keep what I have, attempting to achieve more so I might build up my storehouses of reputation, honor, and a sense deep inside myself that I was not a disappointment.

I wasn't sleeping well. And no wonder, because I felt as if the whole world were waiting for my command! I'd made myself and my abilities bigger than God and his abilities in my own eyes.

God gently took me back to the basics. He took me to creation. I held out my hand and inspected it thoroughly, tracing the veins with my eyes, wiggling my fingers and imagining the bones moving

inside. I thought about how he created me. He created me as flesh
and blood. I'm dirt and dust, and to dust I will return. I didn't make
my heart start beating or put breath in my lungs. I'm not sending
blood pumping through my veins. All that I am, I was given—my
personality, skills, breath, and life. Even the place and time in which
I reside. My husband, Kyle, and our kids are similar miracles, moving and breathing beside me through this life.

Then, perched on the couch, I looked out my window and thought
about how God created everything I could see and how I didn't
understand it fully. How do birds fly? In what way do hydrogen and
oxygen fit together to form water? Sometimes I think I know things,
that I've thought them and understood them on my own, but when
it comes to making and sustaining the simplest parts of this life, the
things I simply take for granted, I know nothing and have no power
to make or sustain anything.

I think maturity means coming to a greater sense of our own
helplessness and powerlessness and at the same time turning to
see how much God is doing and has done—how he is sustaining
our hearts and lungs and the trees and the birds right outside our
window. And how a baby is formed in the secret and how a soul
comes to faith and how love and grace happen. This is why God is
worthy of our allegiance, because he's doing everything and gift-
ing everything, and we're doing nothing but what he's given us to
do—breathing, parenting, ministering, thinking, understanding,
and even believing. How can the self-idolatry of anxiety exist with
that same belief?

King Jesus addressed this same question with people who came
to hear his teaching. He knew their constant pull toward anxiety,
and he knew the lies that were consuming them.

> Therefore I tell you, do not be anxious about your life, what you will
> eat or what you will drink, nor about your body, what you will put
> on. Is not life more than food, and the body more than clothing?

Look at the birds of the air: they neither sow nor reap nor gather into barns, and yet your heavenly Father feeds them. Are you not of more value than they? And which of you by being anxious can add a single hour to his span of life? And why are you anxious about clothing? Consider the lilies of the field, how they grow: they neither toil nor spin, yet I tell you, even Solomon in all his glory was not arrayed like one of these. But if God so clothes the grass of the field, which today is alive and tomorrow is thrown into the oven, will he not much more clothe you, O you of little faith? Therefore do not be anxious, saying, "What shall we eat?" or "What shall we drink?" or "What shall we wear?" For the Gentiles seek after all these things, and your heavenly Father knows that you need them all. But seek first the kingdom of God and his righteousness, and all these things will be added to you.

Therefore do not be anxious about tomorrow, for tomorrow will be anxious for itself. Sufficient for the day is its own trouble. (Matt. 6:25–34)

Jesus tells us many things here, but they all fall under his one command that we should not be anxious.

Easier said than done, Jesus. And all the people said *Amen*.

Thankfully, Jesus gives us excellent reasons why anxiety deserves none (I repeat, *none*) of our allegiance.

First, he says that there are some things we don't need to think about. It's not that we just *shouldn't* think about these things but we *don't need* to think about them—because *someone else is thinking about them for us*. That Someone is God. He's on it. When the responsibilities were meted out, he willingly signed up for the job of provision. He's attentive toward our physical needs for food, water, and clothing. He's attentive toward our emotional needs for value and significance. He's attentive toward our limits of time and space, our todays and tomorrows.

For a Jewish audience who would not breathe God's name out loud because they considered him so high and holy, Jesus uses an interesting word here for God. He says we should think of him as a father and should do so specifically in relation to our anxiety and our needs.

In his letters to the churches, Paul says we shouldn't just *think* of God as a father but should cry out to him for help using the name Dada (Gal. 4:6). Jesus brings our high and lifted up God to a level of affection and intimacy. In other words, he seems to say, "God loves you with a great and protective love, and you can call on him as your Daddy."

I remember awakening from a bad dream as a child. The dream felt so real—as an eight-year-old, I had become orphaned. My parents had died, and I was all alone. When I woke up in a panic, I ran out into the living room where my dad was sitting in his chair watching *Hill Street Blues* or *Cheers* or some other show that ran after my bedtime. When I saw my dad, I suddenly felt ashamed of my childish anxieties and couldn't express my fear to him. But it didn't matter. My father pulled me onto his lap and rocked me back to sleep. In his presence, I felt so completely protected and safe, so safe that at this very moment, as I am typing these words as a forty-two-year-old woman, my eyes fill with tears at the memory. We never grow too old to need protection and care in this broken-down world.

If my imperfect father knew instinctively how to comfort and love me like that, then how does my Father in heaven, sitting on the throne in authority over this world, know how to meet my needs? Perfectly. This is where Jesus draws our attention. He doesn't say that we should look at our imperfect dads—and some of our dads fathered very imperfectly. He says that we should look at the intention of ideal fatherhood—to provide and protect—and know that's who God is.

Second, Jesus uses two people or people groups—Solomon and the gentiles—to help us distinguish where we are. He localizes us. He identifies with Solomon those who fulfill his command to not be anxious, and he identifies with the gentiles those who are anxious. Solomon was a king who built God's temple, literally a place where God reigned and was worshiped. The gentiles are people who don't bow before God; they reject him and are not included in his family.

Jesus is talking kingdom talk here. He's asking his audience to consider their allegiance. Are you bowing with Solomon, or are you with the gentiles? Are you "in Adam" and this kingdom of earth or "in Christ" and a subject of his kingdom? Gentiles don't know how God works; they don't know him as a father, so they anxiously pursue what they need and want. But those who, like Solomon, know they have a God who relates to them as a Father does with his children—they are the ones who know God is not merely attentive to them but is *for them.*

Put Anxiety through the Kingdom Story

Anxiety, then, is misplaced attentiveness. An attentiveness to needs we ourselves are thoroughly unable to fill leaves us, consequentially, with shaky confidence. Anxiety is not productive or powerful to change anything. That's what Jesus says. When we give our minds over to it, however, it feels as if just by thinking about a circumstance we can change it, or that if we worry about the future enough, we can affect or prevent misfortune. Anxiety makes God appear small, uncaring, and untrustworthy—a disengaged or even an absent Father.

The problem isn't that we have needs or questions; the problem comes when we choose to turn in the wrong direction to deal with our concerns.

Jesus teaches us that, as kingdom citizens, we must be attentive to what cultivates a confidence in God. The command in Matthew 6 can be summarized as "Don't attend to what is not your responsibility; do observe and consider what underlines this truth." In other words, we should consistently think about God and all the ways he provides.

Look at the birds. Look at the flowers. Look at the diversity of faces around you. Feel the sun on your skin.

It's just what God reminded me of in my months of worry: *Look at your hands, examine your breath, notice the bird's song as it's perched on the porch railing. Remember who sustains these things. Your security is in this God who provides, and he willingly provides from a place of fatherly love.*

When we choose a wrong attentiveness, we live as functional orphans, those who must fight for what they need and care for themselves, and who respond to life from a place of fear rather than love. Of course this births anxiety, because we know we're but children who *need*. Why would we expect ourselves, as children, to also provide?

The good news about God as Father is that he is constantly engaged and present, and he *chooses* to be so. Our God is one who never needs rest (Isa. 40:28); he is always working, always aware.

So Jesus says to his listeners that we shouldn't be attentive to how our needs may be met but rather to the God who meets our needs. He also delves deeper, questioning us on what we find truly important. In other words, he implies that we should consider what happiness is.

We think we know what will make us happy and what exactly we need, and if we simply attend to these things, all will be well. Are we, however, living for what's actually worth living for? Are we trying to grasp and hold on to things that God himself says are not of utmost value, things like nice clothing and money and the right kinds of food? Is this grasping the source of our anxiety?

Well, yes, yes it is. We've made life about curating a perfect family, the right education, a marital status, granite countertops, political parties, travel experiences, or our Roth IRA.

Jesus doesn't slap our wrist and say, "Just don't think about those things." He wants us to consider that life as it's intended under his rule and reign is not about physical and tangible things we put on or in our body. Jesus is telling us that our *soul* is required of us, so we should seek the kingdom. He points to what matters as if to say, "Be attentive *here* instead."

There are some things to which we should be attentive, truths that will ease our anxiety and fill our heart with confidence toward God. He's already told us one: think of God as our good Father, supplying in love all that we need.

In considering God as Father, we see a second focus coming into view: we must also then think of ourselves as children. We've seen this before; Jesus said that those who enter the kingdom come as children. Thinking of ourselves as children brings our attention to the present day, for children live completely in the present, unable even to conceptualize yesterday and tomorrow and next year. Living according to the kingdom of God means we attend to today, not the "what ifs" or the "what I wants" but the "what is."

In one of my ongoing battles with anxiety related to one of my children, I've repeatedly learned that to consider the near (or far) future always fills me with more worries and questions. I can't conceptualize the future, although I've certainly tried. The "what ifs" of what might become of him has caused me to consider every possible scenario, each finding its end in grief and despair. I finally realized that I'd spent years borrowing grief from the future, worrying and despairing over what might or might not be.

Jesus teaches us by his own example that we should be attentively present in the day we're experiencing. He knew of the beckoning cross all his life, and yet he lounged with his friends over a meal, enjoyed the laughter of hordes of children gathering at his feet, and cultivated deep relationships he knew would be interrupted at the cross. How did he keep anxiety at bay? He lived what he taught us to pray: "Give us this day our daily bread" (Matt. 6:11). He basked in the in-this-day presence of his Father, and he asked his Father for (and relied on) what he needed for that day. He'd do the same on the day he faced his death, the hardest day of his life. He lived without borrowing grief from the future.

But we should absolutely attend to the future. This is the third focus to which Jesus averts our attention: he says we *should* chase down rabbit trails in our mind regarding the kingdom.

Our anxiety will always lead us to tomorrow, next week, and next year, but it never takes us far enough into the future. "The future" to us is what happens within our lifetime. The future Jesus speaks of is the fulfillment of the kingdom. When he says, "Seek first the kingdom," he's reminding us there is an end to this life and to all the clothes and food and money we pine after. Why worry about a misfortune in the future when one day every tear will be wiped away and all things will be made new? Jesus says we should think ahead to the kingdom, precisely so we might keep our perspective in check about what really matters and what's really worth giving our time and mental energy toward. In other words, we should be attentive to our true security: a place in God's family forever, an inheritance that cannot be taken away, and a God who will never fail us and whom we will one day see face-to-face.

As we do this, what will grow? We will experience the peaceful simplicity of not needing to hold on to much of anything in this life, except what actually matters.

It may be easier than we think to decide what does.

"When we have so much to lose, then the fear of losing any of it terrifies," says writer and pastor Winn Collier, with a wise suggestion: "So let's go ahead and lose, lose it all. Let it burn. Then let's move on to the joy. It is our birthright to live as joyful children sustained by the kindness and mercy of our Father. Do not fret. Give way to the grace of losing your life. We are God's dear children. We will be okay."[3]

practicing THE *kingdom* OF *god*

I'd like to suggest some daily practices that God may use to turn your heart away from anxiety and toward its happiest allegiance: Jesus. In all of these, it is not the actual practice that will transform you but rather the Holy Spirit meeting and helping you in them. Look for him, listen for him, and follow his lead in deep reverence for your King.

1. Look and think about what parts of creation are around you. How are these sustained? How do they grow? Wonder at what they teach you about our Creator God, and then consider your role in making, keeping, or growing them. What does this teach you about yourself in relation to God?

2. Write down what is drawing your attention toward anxiety. Look at your list through the lens of the forever kingdom. What about this matters in the long run? Is it the heart of your child or just the way he or she appears to your friends? Is it doing work faithfully in a way that points to the goodness of God or is it just completing a deadline? Is it trying to prevent bad things from happening or trusting and waiting on God to refine your faith in the pain you're feeling? Do you really believe that getting this thing you want—a vacation, a husband or wife, a bigger apartment, a sure future next year—is going to satisfy the deepest longing in your soul and forever ease the struggles you face? Ask God to reorient you around kingdom priorities: "For the kingdom of

God is not a matter of eating and drinking but of righteousness and peace and joy in the Holy Spirit" (Rom. 14:17).

3. Practice thinking in the present. When you sense your thoughts drawing away to the immediate future, refuse to go down the rabbit trails. Bring your attention back by considering God's character and how he in his character is present with you today. He is faithful. He is a good Father who knows your need. He is accessible and ready to receive your concerns through prayer. He won't ever leave you. *You are not an orphan; it's not up to you.* As you practice keeping your thoughts throughout the day in the present, pray, "Give me this day my daily bread." Believe by faith that he is helping you.

4. Practice preventive attentiveness. Anxiety is often a monologue of sporadic thoughts. Bring God into your thoughts, making it a dialogue, allowing him to challenge your thoughts with what is true. We do this through the consistent study of God's Word. Invite God to speak as you open your Bible. Make daily deposits of truth.

5. Enact the "we" of the kingdom. If you are consistently struggling with misplaced attentiveness, confess your sin to someone who will offer you wise counsel and biblical truth. If you have done battle with anxiety and have learned a few things along the way, how can you share your story with others? How can you come alongside someone who is currently struggling?

6. Often our tendency toward misplaced allegiance has, at its root, a clue about how God has made us. A person tending toward anxiety is perhaps a person imprinted with compassion, sensitivity, and deep awareness. With properly aligned allegiance, this is a person who displays the fruit of peace that can only come from the Holy Spirit. Ask him to grow this fruit in you. And consider: How might God, if you live submitted to him, use you and your Spirit-gifted peace in his kingdom?

SIX

image

A young mom asked if she could pick my brain over coffee about rearing boys. I have three of them and she has two, and because I'd survived the little years intact, I suppose she thought I had all the answers.

I had all the answers until I had the actual children, but nonetheless I agreed to the date, and soon after we sat together on a coffee-stained couch. She turned to me with a hint of desperation in her eyes and said, "Tell me how to raise these boys."

These boys were, at that very moment, wrestling each other to the ground in a cordoned off area for kids in the coffee shop. That is to say, they were doing as boys often do: playing rough and tumble, loudly enjoying themselves, and incessantly calling for their mother to watch them jump from some high ledge with a mischievous smile on their faces.

These were my boys in miniature, and I smiled as I reflected on the chaotic, tiring, wonderful years when my three were smaller.

Tell me how to raise these boys. I could tell by the way she asked for my advice that what she really wanted was some sort of formula—some *magic* formula—that would, if implemented flawlessly, produce well-behaved, well-rounded young men. Throw in a little family devotional time, a sprinkling of patient discipline, a dollop of the perfect schooling choice, mix them with the right words at the right moment, and *voilà*, you've got yourself a God-fearing man.

Perhaps I read into her question a little too much—I know she genuinely wants to be a good mom. But I too once sat with an older woman and asked the same question. I too have been the mom looking for a formula.

I remember the humiliation and anger I felt when my oldest son melted down for the first time as we were going into the grocery store. On the sidewalk, in the exact place the sliding doors whooshed open and shut for shoppers, my son decided he didn't care to grocery shop that day. He much preferred his trains waiting for him in the car or his toys at home or any other option aside from traipsing through the aisles for milk and bread. To announce his preference, he threw himself onto the concrete and wailed as if I were torturing him. Each time I tried to set him on his feet, he went boneless,[1] refusing to stand but continuing to scream bloody murder. There, on the store threshold, it seemed as if everyone in the entire universe stopped and stared, gaping not at him but rather at *me*. Apparently they wanted to get a good, long look at the worst mother in the world.

I pretended I didn't see their stares. I pretended I knew exactly how to parent this tantrum away. I pretended I was calm, cool, and collected, but inside I was convinced they were right. I *wasn't* a good mom, because good moms don't have children who behave in such a way. Clearly, I needed to up my game.

So, yes, I've been the mom looking for a magic formula.

Scratch that.

I *am* the mom looking for the formula. I'm the girl looking to somehow unlock the perfect life. I have a deeply ingrained fear of "getting it wrong," so I find myself chasing after every little thing that seems "right"—the right way of interacting with social media, the right amount of screen time for my kids, the right opportunities for serving, the right spiritual disciplines, the right way to be a pastor's wife, the right place in God's will, the right choices for myself and those in my circle of influence. It's exhausting trying to get it right in every area of my life.

But here's an important question I've recognized I need to consistently consider: Can a formula or the "right" behaviors reach inside and actually change a heart? Can I change the hearts of my children with the correct amount of family devotional time?

I imagine trying to reach down deep inside my children and flip a switch in them, turning off ungodliness and turning on righteousness, and I see the absurdity of it all. I'm absolutely powerless to change *myself* in the places it really matters, as powerless as I was to make my spiritual heart beat when I was dead in my sins.

So why do I believe I can change the hearts of my children with a formula?

An Allegiance to Delusion

This is an important question to consider, because the heart is where God's eyes are, and his entire interest is in our heart being undivided and fully aligned with his. If we believe a formula or completed checklist is the way to that spiritual maturity, we're not concerned with who God is. We're instead placing great faith in our own power and abilities, believing external behaviors can alter internal realities. The apostle Paul says this sort of striving, although meant to please God or exhibit a devotion to him, actually happens apart from him. He says it's foolish to think we who experienced the beginning of the Christian life by the Spirit's supernatural work can then perfect ourselves by our own external efforts (Gal. 3:3). This is a consequential misunderstanding of the gospel and a form of religious delusion. It is instead an allegiance to image maintenance.

This false king of image is powerful because it's subtle, it makes us look so very good on the outside, and it tweaks and twists the true words of King Jesus. When we lack discernment, or when we don't know the gospel, we believe this false allegiance is actually what allegiance to Jesus looks like. In fact, it's the *anti-gospel*.

The work of the kingdom of God happens from the inside out, starting with Jesus's rule in our heart. Jesus's rule transforms us, giving us new motivations, understanding, and character—things that automatically manifest themselves in our external practices. In other words, Jesus's rule in our heart cannot help but show.

If all we're concerned with is our behavior or how we appear to others, we want the manifestation of a transformation that's not actually happened, so we end up trying to manufacture spiritual realities with behaviors and disciplines.

There is a more devious reason for focusing on external behaviors, however. If we're *pretending* to be concerned with matters of the heart, going through certain religious motions in order to present a certain image to others, it's not that we're just not concerned with what God is concerned with, as if we've gotten slightly distracted; it's that we're *using* God to gain our own self-glory. We're perfectly fine to continue down roads pockmarked with sin, as long as our path stays hidden from those we most want to impress or hide from.

In both cases, we don't want God. We simply want to maintain an illusion of spirituality. Even if our intentions are good, even if we attempt by good behavior to earn our spiritual growth, we at some level must pretend away our besetting sins or hide self-protectively from true gospel community that is solidified through confession, repentance, and forgiveness.

An allegiance to King Image is ultimately an allegiance to delusion, to spiritual smoke and mirrors.

I know this allegiance so well myself. In fact, I lived the majority of my Christian life giving allegiance to the delusion that I could fix myself and everyone else around me. If I were disciplined enough, if I served enough, if I willed and worked away my sin, I would reach a level of unmatched spiritual maturity. I was determined to be a "good girl," but my so-called goodness masked layers of pride, fear, hidden sin, and despair over my glaring inability to be the good Christian I knew I must be in order to be approved by God.

I look back now and see how I was under deep condemnation. The false allegiance to image urged me to do something about my sin and to provide my own spiritual security and comfort. I couldn't actually confess my sin or admit my spiritual poverty, because the image I held of myself would take a hit. So instead I attempted to make up for my failures and cover them over. I vowed to do better the next time—the mantra of one giving allegiance to image. Sometimes I did do better the next time, but then I would fail and the cycle would begin again. This allegiance is a jail of condemnation, always reminding me I am weak and unable to be perfect but never providing a solution other than "try harder."

I was spiritually stunted, and because I hadn't experienced true transformation at the heart level, I became the biggest pretender of them all. Knowing the truth about myself, I hid.

American evangelicalism is overrun with pretenders, Christians who say with their lips that they live their lives for Jesus but who are more concerned with rules, checklists, categories, appearance, protecting secret sins, or aligning with the "right" people and "right" causes on social media. We look much like our Instagram-soaked world, where what we present to others for consumption is intended to build a personal brand and is only a slight representation of our real life, much less our real hearts.

In other words, it's easy to hide these days.

And in hiding, we protect all manner of trouble that King Jesus wants to shine his blazing light on for our healing.

The Real Image

Why was I so humiliated that day at the grocery store when my son threw himself down on the ground? Every parent instinctively knows why: because people saw it! My son's tantrum revealed not only his defiance but also my own belief that his behavior reflected on my success as a parent. I could not, I supposed, be a good parent if my child acted this way.

But good parenting is more than putting a child through his paces in a grocery store aisle. A child is still considered immature and rebellious if he or she outwardly obeys a parent but does so with a defiant attitude. The heart must align with the behavior in order for the child to truly be obedient to parental authority.

It's easy to grasp this truth in regard to our children—we spend their childhoods training their insides to match their outsides. When it comes to our own heart, however, we much prefer the charade of being mismatched. We forget that God not only sees our inside with laser clarity but that this is actually the place where he attributes either holiness or unrighteousness.

Jesus tried to get people to understand this. As he traveled, proclaiming the kingdom of God, he often pointed to the Pharisees as who *not* to be like. This must have befuddled the listening crowds, because in that time, the Pharisees were the primary point of reference when it came to spiritual standards of holiness. The Pharisees were the religious elite, the respected minority, the ultimate models of devotion to God. They showed this devotion by stridently focusing on avoiding what would defile them outwardly and on doing all the "right" activities for their neighbors to see.

Jesus, knowing their hearts, pointed out how they prayed loudly and elaborately, not for the ears of God but in order to garner the admiration of people. They only went through their ritualistic motions if someone was watching, and they wanted everyone to know of their practices and good works. The religious checklist was alive and well.

The Pharisees specifically confronted Jesus about his failure to engage in their hand-washing rituals. He showed a scandalous lack of concern for their manmade rules.

Then Pharisees and scribes came to Jesus from Jerusalem and said, "Why do your disciples break the tradition of the elders? For they do not wash their hands when they eat." He answered them, "And why do you break the commandment of God for the sake of your tradition? . . . You hypocrites! Well did Isaiah prophesy of you, when he said:

> 'This people honors me with their lips,
>> but their heart is far from me;
> in vain do they worship me,
>> teaching as doctrines the commandments of men.'"
> (Matt. 15:1–9)

In other words, their insides and outsides were mismatched. They followed the rules but entirely missed the heart behind the commandments God had given. They were like a child who, on errands with her mother, went where she was directed but on the inside seethed with bitter defiance.

So Jesus used the Pharisees and scribes as an object lesson.

[Jesus] called the people to him and said to them, "Hear and understand: it is not what goes into the mouth that defiles a person, but what comes out of the mouth; this defiles a person. . . . Do you not see that whatever goes into the mouth passes into the stomach and is expelled? But what comes out of the mouth proceeds from the heart, and this defiles a person. For out of the heart come evil thoughts, murder, adultery, sexual immorality, theft, false witness, slander. These are what defile a person. But to eat with unwashed hands does not defile anyone. (vv. 10–11, 17–20)

Jesus communicated that religious practices don't always flow from a holy heart, and that anyone who truly wants to show wholehearted allegiance to God should be deeply concerned with true defilement—an unrighteous heart. An unrighteous heart leads to unrighteous acts, but a righteous heart will produce true obedience.

We innately believe we can hide or pretend or fake devotion, and we often can for a time, but eventually who we really are on the inside is revealed. In fact, Jesus said as much: "Beware of the leaven of the Pharisees, which is hypocrisy. Nothing is covered up that will not be revealed, or hidden that will not be known" (Luke 12:1–2).

Our heart will be exposed one day, perhaps in this age but certainly in the age to come. So we must not fear humankind and its rules. We must not spend one moment pretending or going through the religious motions in order to project a certain image. We must instead fear God and follow in his ways.

I hear an invitation in Jesus's words: we can either continue living in delusion or ask God to hold a mirror up to our heart in order to show us the reality of who we are and enable us to respond accordingly. A continued allegiance to delusion keeps our secret sins hidden from others, yes, but they also remain unhealed by God. It keeps us glued to a religious checklist but also spiritually stunted. We'll never truly know what it means to have faith or to walk by the Spirit, and we'll never know the true forgiveness and freedom that only the Spirit of God can give.

Delusion or reality? Which do you want?

I'm not suggesting that seeing the reality of who we are before God or confessing what we see there to others is a cakewalk. I am suggesting, however, that if we truly desire an intimate, unencumbered relationship with God, what we really desire is stark, laid-bare reality. God can work with reality; in fact, he *delights* when we embrace reality, for when we do, we're simply agreeing with him in confession and repentance that we are spiritually bankrupt and unable to make our hearts holy. He then floods our helpless, thirsty hearts with his mercy and grace and gladly begins the lifelong process of matching our outside to our holy inside.

God is not afraid of the reality of what's in our hearts. He's not impatient, angry, or slow in offering us mercy. He knows how we're formed; he knows we are but dust (Ps. 103:14). Jesus even says that when we acknowledge our human state, only then are we blessed by God and handed his kingdom (Matt. 5:3).

Healing comes when we bring our secrets into the light, when we stop going through our religious rituals and manufacturing our image and instead *receive* the King and his kingdom. His offer of peace and joy—even in those deep, secret places we hope to pretend away—is not smoke and mirrors. It's a very real promise.

The question for us then becomes what Jesus asked the invalid who'd lain by the pool for thirty-eight years, trying to make it to the waters when they stirred, "Do you want to be healed?" (see John 5:1–8).

Do you actually want healing for the sin or hurt you've held for years?

Do you actually want restoration?

Do you actually want to experience God's grace and love?

Do you actually want to walk closely with your God?

Do you actually want your inside and outside to match?

The minute you acknowledge you can't do any of this for yourself (and by any of this, I mean the entire Christian life) and that you need Jesus for it all, the minute that you confess and repent, the kingdom of God rushes in by the Holy Spirit to clean, excise sin, and begin to match your outside with your regenerated inside.

You'll know that God has made a way for you, and you'll never want delusion again.

Holy Secrecy

Jesus pointed at the Pharisees and the scribes as an illustration, teaching us we must not pray and fast with empty words and false motivations beneath the surface (Matt. 6:5). We shouldn't do good works in public while our hearts hide sinful secrets.

We should, however, practice *holy* secrecy. Our King says we're to do good works secretly, before the eyes of God alone, unconcerned about whether or not they're seen by others (vv. 3–4). We're to pray in secret, speaking simple and honest words to God (v. 6). We're to fast without anyone knowing, remembering that God receives our devotion (vv. 17–18). We're to store up treasures in the secret places of heaven—the places we can't see yet—which we in fact do through our holy secrecy (v. 20).

How do we practice this holy secrecy? How do we cultivate a love to move in and among the places where God sees but others don't?

We train ourselves to look in the correct mirror.

As a teenager, I didn't need to be trained to look at my reflection in the mirror before leaving the house. I spent an inordinate amount of time in front of a mirror, manipulating the height of my bangs and scrunching my perm to perfection. I was constantly adjusting my clothes, inspecting my skin for imperfections, and checking my teeth.

I didn't need training, but apparently boys do. Two of my three boys simply do not ever look at themselves in the mirror. They may occasionally run a comb through their hair, but they don't check their work while doing so. I'm constantly sending them back to the bathroom to see the reality of the bird's nest hair they woke up with or the toothpaste that dried on their cheek from the previous night's brushing.

My hope is that, by seeing, they will adjust themselves accordingly. They'll see how navy and black don't match, and they'll change. They'll see the stain on their clothes, and they'll change. Most of the time they don't care, but I promise, potential future daughters-in-law, I'm trying!

I'm training them that mirrors aren't merely for vanity. A mirror reflects back to us the reality of what we look like, so we can make adjustments accordingly.

The Pharisees and scribes were addicted to the mirror of others, and they based their identity on what others reflected back to them. They positioned and adjusted themselves so they would be considered devout, holy, and close to God. They were considered good people who should lead, teach others, and be others' example of piety. Their outward behaviors earned them these commendations.

Unfortunately, the mirror they used didn't reflect God's perspective back to them. Jesus could not commend them. Instead he called them whitewashed tombs, cleaned up on the outside but spiritually dead on the inside.

What mirrors are we looking into in order to determine who we are and whether or not we're valuable? What commendations do we hope others will reflect back onto us? And what will we do in order to be commended in such a way? We will do just about anything and so often do so without any awareness of what we're doing. We end up in a fun house with distorted mirrors and, therefore, distorted minds and hearts.

We need a mirror that reflects reality, and praise be to God, we have it in the holy Scriptures.

God's mirror doesn't reflect an outward representation, however. His mirror shows what's in the heart of every person. When we look at our reflection in the Word, we see the reality of who we are and how desperately we need our King. We see how holy he is, and then we adjust ourselves accordingly. We reject delusion, seeking to match our outside with the inside reality of what God has done in our heart:

But be doers of the word, and not hearers only, deceiving yourselves. For if anyone is a hearer of the word and not a doer, he is like a man who looks intently at his natural face in a mirror. For he looks at himself and goes away and at once forgets what he was like. (James 1:22–24)

Again, God never requires of us without promising he'll also give. When we give ourselves to holy secrecy, training ourselves to look in the mirror of God's Word, what gift do we then receive? "But the one who looks into the perfect law, the law of liberty, and perseveres, being no hearer who forgets but a doer who acts, *he will be blessed in his doing*" (v. 25, emphasis mine).

We're blessed in our doing.

In other words, we discover a unique joy in our internal, not-seen-by-others works, because the proper motivation undergirds them. The inside matches the outside—a formula, if you will, for peace and joy.

The mirror of God's Word is key. Often when we have an allegiance to image, we're like teenage boys: we're not even looking in the mirror. We have no desire for God's Word, no interest in what God wants us to see there, and we're certainly not concerned with making tweaks and adjustments.

However, in order to break this allegiance to image, we must train ourselves to look in the mirror of God's Word. Training involves discipline; if we wait for the desire to do so, we'll be waiting indefinitely. Desire most often is a *fruit* of training—as we persevere (the word James uses), we experience the benefits and joys of the training, and we want to continue. Another name for "want to" is *desire*.

In the years I lived with an allegiance to image, I read my Bible. I approached it, however, not as a mirror but rather as an ATM machine. Sometimes I read it so I could pat myself on the back in smug satisfaction, because Scripture reading was at the top of my Good Christian checklist, and I'd done my duty for the day. At other times I read it because I needed a shot of feel-better. I withdrew a verse or two of comfort from Scripture as I'd withdraw money from the ATM. This approach was based upon feelings and desire: when

I wanted (and didn't want) to do it, what I wanted (and didn't want) from it, and what I wanted (and didn't want) to read. An approach to Scripture based upon feelings, however, will never produce spiritual maturity. We will remain in our delusion.

To approach the Bible as a mirror, however, puts our feelings and desires in submission to God. We bring ourselves to God, laying ourselves bare to him through the disciplined reading and study of his Word. When we're systematic and thoughtful in our approach, we're allowing God access to speak when he wants to speak, convict when he wants to convict, encourage when he wants to encourage, and teach when he wants to teach. In other words, when we show up, day after day, to intently gaze into truth, he does the work of showing us where we need to adjust our emotions, thoughts, and behaviors, and he reminds us through his Word that the Holy Spirit is the leading agent for our change.

Why must we engage the Word of God in secret? Why does Jesus highlight holy secrecy? Why is it not enough that we engage it corporately, such as in the hearing of a sermon or in a group Bible study?

Because when we see the reality of our heart, we will at times lament and grieve, and this sort of grieving needs space and concentrated thought. Mostly we need an opportunity to hear the quiet whisper of forgiveness and hope from the Holy Spirit as reflected back to us in the mirror of Scripture. Hearing what another person has digested is not the same as hearing truth and digesting it ourselves. The Holy Spirit will convict and apply the truth of the Word individually in our heart as we come to it privately. Most importantly, when striving and activity and noise cease, we're left only with God himself, and he is ultimately whom we need to meet with and hear from.

We receive the blessing and correction of the kingdom in personal relationship with the King.

If we want to grow, that is.

Again the question surfaces: Do you want to be healed?

Then go into the secret and meet God there. God brings gifts to your meeting. He delights in bringing comfort to those who mourn (Matt. 5:4) where their sin has taken them, freedom to those who are captive and brokenhearted (Isa. 61:1–3), and healing to those who long for restoration. He comforts us with the reminder that we do not in fact have to maintain a certain image—for him or anyone else—but that he's received us into the kingdom of God and given us everything we need for life and godliness (2 Pet. 1:3). Perhaps most comforting of all, he will help us become more like our King. He who began a good work in us will complete it (Phil. 1:6).

This comfort is the gift God gives in our secret meetings with him.

But there is more that happens there.

Holy secrecy becomes seen in all the right ways.

Rising Joy

Let us return to the initial question: Can a formula change a heart? Can the external change internal realities?

Only the Spirit of God can change a heart, so if we want our heart transformed to reflect the holiness and goodness of our King, we must cultivate holy secrecy, meeting with God and responding to what his Word reflects back to us.

Certainly, this will at various points include spiritual disciplines such as prayer, fasting, and memorizing Scripture. We will attend church and perhaps a Bible study or small group. But it is not the act of doing these things that changes our heart; it is the Spirit of God working through the sermon or time of Bible study that pierces our heart and helps us apply the truths we're hearing or reading. These activities are good but they are simply ways we place ourselves in the secret with God. We say to God through these practices, "Here I am, listening."

The Holy Spirit changes us in ways that are mysterious and immeasurable. You'll know you've met with him when, over time and through consistently depositing the Word into your heart, you discover an unmanufactured joy rising in you. This is the reward Jesus speaks of when he encourages us to practice holy secrecy: "And your Father who sees in secret will reward you" (Matt. 6:4, 6, 18). He rewards with joy and with his presence with you there in the secret.

False Christianity, based upon the mirrors of religion or others, is depressing because it produces miserable people who worry about self and their little actions and sins, forever weighing themselves on a moving scale. There is no true reward when we give our allegiance to image.

The kingdom of God is internal and claims rule over us in the secret, but it always bears the fruit of righteousness externally. In other words, Holy Spirit–produced joy cannot be contained. He makes us salt and light in the world (5:13–14), eager to do what's right and good, eager to shout from the rooftops what God's whispered to us in secret (10:27), not so we can maintain some sort of image or receive adulation but rather so God can receive glory. So we may be praying or ministering where people can see, but we're only looking at God's smile reflected back to us as we do so.

When the young mom of boys asked her question, she waited on the edge of her chair, expectant for my response. I knew my answer was going to disappoint her, because it wasn't a formula or a step-by-step list. This is what I said: "The most important priority for you as a mom is to walk with God daily and listen for his leadership. He will lead you as you lead these boys. He knows what they need, and he'll guide you to what is right and best for them."

Of course I could have spoken about discipline strategies or best practices, but I said instead what I knew she needed to hear—because it's what I need to hear every day.

Everything external must come first from a sure internal reality.

And it happens daily, in the secret, when the King whispers it into our heart through his Word.

practicing THE *kingdom* OF *god*

As before, I'd like to suggest some daily practices that God may use to turn your heart away from pretending and toward its happiest allegiance: Jesus. Remember, in all these practices, it is not the actual practice that will transform you but rather the Holy Spirit meeting and helping you in them. Look for him, listen for him, and follow his lead in deep reverence for your King.

1. Plan to get alone at some point this week for an hour. In that hour, remove all distractions and answer these questions in a journal: *Can I change my heart? Can I change the hearts of those I love?* In what ways are you relying on checklists, formulas, or other external behaviors to either change or hide internal realities? Finally, consider if you want reality rather than delusion. Jesus asks you, as he did the invalid, "Do you want to be healed?"

2. Enact the "we" of the kingdom. Because you've pretended, this will be extremely challenging, but it's exactly what you need. Go to a trusted friend who will likely respond with both truth and grace and confess where you are. Confess what you're doing only for others to see. Confess what on your outside doesn't match your inside. Confess, if needed, your confusion about God's Word or lack of discipline in studying the Bible. Ask your friend for help in learning to study the Bible.

3. Practice holy secrecy. Do a good work without telling anyone else about it, doing it only "before the eyes of God." After doing so, consider what you've learned about your motivations.

4. Practice the holy secrecy of meeting with God. Choose a time and place where you'll bring yourself to God's Word each day this week. If you don't know where to start, begin reading in Psalm 1. Read a psalm each day, looking for one characteristic about God you can meditate on. For example, you may read that God is your refuge. Think about that. What does it mean to have a refuge? What does this say about who God is? And what does this say about who you are and how you're to relate to God?

5. Often the area in which we have a tendency toward misplaced allegiance has, at its root, a clue about how God has made us. A person tending toward image is perhaps a person who is an accomplisher or leader. With properly aligned allegiance, this is a person who displays the fruit of goodness that can only come from the Holy Spirit. Ask him to grow this fruit in you. And consider: How might God, if you live submitted to him, use you and your Spirit-gifted goodness in his kingdom?

6. For further reading: Matthew 23, Matthew 6:1–24, James 1:22–25, Psalm 1, and Hebrews 4:12.

SEVEN

control

After nineteen years of marriage, the relationship patterns between Kyle and me have become so ingrained they are practically immortalized in concrete. I suppose this is true in any long-term relationship, whether it be friends or an adult daughter returning to her childhood home for a holiday with her parents. Whether they're right or wrong, healthy or unhealthy, we easily fall back into familiar relationship patterns without conscious thought or awareness.

Yesterday I sat opposite my husband on our couch, and we dissected aspects of our marriage and how we each can grow. By God's grace, I saw for the very first time a solidified pattern I'd carried into every interaction with him since we started dating: I'm afraid to ask for what I want, but I want what I want nonetheless. *He* has done nothing to make me afraid; Kyle is in fact the kindest, most servant-hearted person I know. Ironically, it's my own tight grip on control that's made me afraid. I generally know what I want, but to ask for it outright is to trust Kyle won't invalidate my thoughts, which, of course, in my mind means invalidating my very existence. I fear going unseen, forgotten—withering away under the needs and desires of others—but actually voicing my perspective or asserting myself makes me vulnerable to rejection or being thought "wrong."

In other words, if I maintain control, I protect myself.

In some sense, that's true. I *do* protect myself. But protecting oneself is not an ingredient for a strong, intimate marriage.

When I recognized the pattern, I realized that all along I'd believed my indirectness was somehow good. It made me a good wife, always the helper, never expecting help. *Whatever you want, dear. I'm here to support and serve you, dear.*

This, however, hasn't served my husband well at all. This pattern has instead cultivated an ongoing guessing game between us. Kyle must guess what I want without me asking for it outright. And then when he doesn't get it right, I claim he doesn't "get me" and punish him for it with a flare of emotion or an unwarranted accusation.

Now, I learned long ago he cannot read my mind, and that telling him how I'd like to be shown love doesn't remove the sincerity from his actions. Apparently, however, I'd gone only further underground, becoming less obvious but maintaining the destabilizing unfairness. Unfairness, because Kyle is called by God to serve and love me as Christ loves the church, but I'd made it incredibly difficult for him to know *how* he could specifically do so.

My self-protection has kept me much more aware of my own needs than his, an excellent scorekeeper, and at the same time fearful and distrustful that my husband will actually look out for me. I am quick to consider what I want and reluctant to serve without first thinking of how I hope to be served in return.

Ultimately, however, it's not that I don't trust Kyle; it's that I don't trust God.

I don't trust that God will meet my needs. I don't trust that God "gets me," or that he's got his eye on where I am or his mind on where I'm headed. I don't trust his authority and sovereignty are *good* authority and sovereignty, and so I hold the world on my tight and anxious shoulders. I prepare for the future like doomsday preppers plan for the economy to tank—storing up energy so this introvert can survive, trying to "live in the present" just in case crisis awaits me around the bend, worrying that my best days are behind me. The weight of my true need feels heavy, but I carry it stoically.

This explains the pattern of my marriage and relationships. Because I don't trust God to meet my needs, I use my needs to play hide-and-seek with those I love most. I secretly want them to notice and rush to my side when I need help, but I'm afraid if I'm too direct, they'll say I'm expecting too much. Because I don't trust God, I put too much stock in what others do for me, but their inevitable imperfection buries me deep inside myself. I maintain tight control over whether or not I can be hurt, and on what I will or won't give away. At the same time, I find myself thinking about who in my church is serving me and how well, how many are following (read: serving) me on social media, and how I can gain more influence and authority in more and more spheres of life.

And so, having a weak view of God's authority, I trust myself, which is to say: I love control. I will do anything to get it, protect it, maintain it. Control is something I hoard because it represents power.

Our Allegiance to Power

These things are embarrassing to admit, but I'm telling you because this is a pattern thriving in our lives and in our modern-day evangelical culture. When we don't trust God as our good Sovereign, our fear regarding an unstable future causes us to turn toward other powers, searching for control and equilibrium. When we don't trust God as our good authority, we inflate our own abilities and seek power and influence through career advancement, money accruement, and aligning with the "right" people. We offer our allegiance to leaders and institutions that promise us the outcomes we most desire.

In the evangelical culture, we're seeing this play out in various ways.

One is in the constant encouragement to pursue our dreams. We're told God would have us do "big things" for his kingdom. What we often equate with "big things" is being seen for what we do, known for what we've built, and accumulating a large platform that feeds our cult of celebrity. Of course, being ambitious for the kingdom of God isn't necessarily wrong, but in our push to pursue our dreams, the true reason or motivation we do so doesn't always translate, and we rarely question whether or not the dream is God-given or God-driven. We simply start with what outcomes we want and work backward from there.

I myself have felt this pull. As a writer, I want my words to have an impact. But why? Am I writing so my name will be known or so I can make lots of money or so I can have influence? At times these motivations have driven me, but when they have, I've noticed that I am wholly unsatisfied in the daily work of writing. I want shortcuts to my desired outcomes, and the outcomes I want in those moments have nothing to do with spotlighting God. They have everything to do with enhancing me. Pursuing my dreams can easily become synonymous with control.

Pursuing our dreams and fulfilling a God-given calling may at times appear similar, but they aren't. I can write for myself, or I can write for God. One is about accumulating power and influence and the other is about giving it away.

Another primary way we see an allegiance to power playing out among Christians is our allegiance to political or national power. In the United States, for example, we seek the fulfillment of our desired outcomes in our laws or through our leaders. We want "our" people to be in power, no matter which party we favor. Just as dreams aren't necessarily bad, government is not either, but when we make politics our ultimate hope, we tend to dilute our kingdom citizenship for the sake of being proximate to power. Our emotions and hopes rise and fall with whichever political party currently holds power; we depend on them to make life feel under control.

Jesus never said his kingdom would come through the power of humankind or the national arrangements of that power. In other words, there is a Power over all earthly powers, and any authority only comes when it's given by God. We bow to him alone.

It's easy to examine an allegiance to power in the church or in the culture at large; it's much more difficult to recognize it in our own lives. Our allegiance to control often shows itself, however, in the intersection of where we have God-given authority and where we experience the most stress. This intersection is what we call *responsibility*. Perhaps you oversee a handful of employees, you manage the checkbook, you have influence in your high school, or you pastor a church. What are you specifically responsible for? And how do you manage that responsibility? That will tell you where your allegiance lies.

The weightiest responsibility I have is being a mother to three boys. I've been given authority by God to parent, train, disciple, and love them, and because I want to parent well, mothering is often my greatest source of stress. Parenting is hard and constant work. Once I feel like I've figured out one stage of parenthood, they go and change on me. Parenting is a long game, full of opportunities to second-guess myself and make mistakes. I hold these precious lives in my hands, and I am one of two primary authorities in their lives. I want to get this right!

So often, however, I manage my responsibility by relying on control. I believe with all sincerity that if I take the right actions at the right time using the right words, I can produce a fully formed adult. Similarly, if I *don't* take the right actions at the right time using the right words, my children are in real danger of going irretrievably off course.

I feel the pressure of perfection in managing myself, my boys, and our lives, but when I consider *why* it's so pressure-filled, I realize I have specific outcomes in mind for them. When I rely on control, when I prepare and plan and buffer everything for them, when I demand they fit my predetermined molds, I'm building my own little kingdom here in this house of mine. There is nothing wrong with wanting to do right by my children, but I do not reign. I must mother my children from an understanding that God reigns, and he reigns well.

Your responsibility and stress may look different from mine, but when we give our allegiance to King Control we are exhibiting a belief that we are more responsible and more capable than God himself is. We confuse God's authority with our own, elevating our personal kingdom and diminishing God's perfect rule and reign.

We don't trust God can or will meet our needs, so we have to do it ourselves.

This is an alluring illusion of power and control.

Rest as Reveling in God

As Creator, God is in control of all he has made, and he exerts his authority with wisdom, goodness, and faithfulness. Because of his faithful service, the Father has rewarded Jesus by enthroning him as King. Jesus is bringing his kingdom even now through the ongoing work of the Holy Spirit. The Godhead rules and reigns perfectly, sustaining and renewing and saving us from the destruction and bondage of self-rule. The kingdom of God, in other words, is the *power* of God.

So when we sing worship songs about giving God control, or we talk about relinquishing control of our lives to him, we're voicing untruths about who we are, who God is, and where we are in his story. We don't hand authority over to God. We don't let Jesus take the wheel, or anything else for that matter.

We never had control to begin with.

We don't determine our days or our outcomes. Any authority or decisions we're given have been shared with us by God. We are dependent creatures from birth to the grave, and this isn't something to overcome or fight against. It's something to revel and rest in, for we live by the power of God, and he is so steady and consistent that he's called faithful and true.

We aren't expected to build a kingdom in God's name and certainly not in our own name. We're invited to come into his kingdom, under his power and authority, and find there that the burden of responsibility is light.

Nothing showcases our allegiance to control like the matter of rest. Our bodies won't let us go without physical rest, but I'm referring to mental, emotional, and spiritual rest. We struggle to set work aside (there's always something more to do), we think the Sabbath is for everyone else but us (look at all we're responsible for), and we push every human limit we have (because having an overscheduled calendar is the new status symbol). It's what we do in practice that tells what we believe, and our lack of rest tells plenty about us.

Kyle and I have had the opportunity to speak to pastors and their wives about this very subject, and we've received more pushback in this area than any other. Pastors are some of the worst offenders when it comes to taking time off, as are leaders or caretakers of any sort. They believe they can't ever stop—the needs are too great. The needs *are* great, but none of us is the Savior. When we try to achieve kingdom cultivation apart from Jesus and the ways he's created us, what we're really seeking is a godlike power. We try in our constant motion to erase our humanness and our inabilities. We try to control.

Rest is a way of practicing the kingdom of God, because when we lay down our work, our caretaking, and our physical motion, it requires trust that our God will do as he says he will: rule and reign without pause. We entrust that the work and the power to cultivate significant kingdom work ultimately belongs to God. We proclaim with a day off or with a nap that Jesus is King and that we belong to his kingdom. Work, of course, can proclaim the same. But control doesn't.

Hiding in the Power of God

As a child, I was extremely shy. When an adult spoke to me or I felt overwhelmed in a social situation, I hid behind my mother, arms gripped tight around her leg, eyes down. I hoped that by doing so, she'd speak for me. I felt sure in her ability to manage any situation, so I hid myself in her ability.

My mother taught me I should look adults in the eye and respond appropriately, and eventually I became more self-assured, but according to Jesus we must learn to be a child again, hiding in his power.

Do you notice a theme concerning the kingdom of God? We are children in the kingdom, and children intuitively know they are dependent and under another's authority. Who they are, how they define themselves, and how they view life are each defined by their relationship to their authority, which makes them vulnerable and explains why Jesus spoke so harshly against the misuse of this authority. A child brings neither power nor true possessions to the parent; they can only give themselves in dependent relationship.

This is exactly what is required of a child of God. It is an invitation, really, to hide in the benevolent power of God. This means, of course, that the concerns of our earthly kingdom—control, influence, and measurable outcomes—cannot be our concerns nor how we measure our value. We can't rely on our own abilities or strength. Doing so obstructs the way of true life in the kingdom.

The kingdom of God does have its concerns, however. Children are dependent and under another's authority, but they are still responsible for their attitudes, behaviors, and the ways in which they relate to their family members. They are given responsibilities, even more so as they grow and mature.

Likewise, as children in the kingdom, we're to pursue what we've been given responsibility for by our King. So we must ask, What is our responsibility in the family of God? And what burdens belong solely to the head of the family—God himself? These are the key questions we must continually keep at the forefront of our minds, because so often we attempt to snatch God's responsibilities from him while ignoring our true responsibilities.

Considering the attributes of God helps us answer the questions. Any attribute or behavior that begins with "omni" or "all" can only be attributed to God: he is omnipresent, omniscient, and of course omnipotent, meaning he is everywhere at once, all knowing, and limitless in power. We are not expected to imitate these characteristics of God, although we often act as if we're capable of doing so and declare with our allegiance to control that we're self-sovereign. We'd like to tell God what to do, not the other way around.

God has other attributes, however, that *are* communicable: he is holy, all-loving, and righteous. We are called to be holy as he is holy (1 Pet. 1:16), to love as he has loved us (1 John 4:11), and to pursue righteousness and godliness (1 Tim. 6:11). Just as a parent says to his or her child, "This is who we are and how we do things in this family," our responsibility as a kingdom child is to cultivate a family resemblance, and in doing so bring honor to our Father.

Knowing our responsibilities in light of God's responsibilities keeps our allegiance on Christ. We recognize how little control we have, how vast God's sovereignty is, and how much we need the power of Christ's Spirit enabling us to fulfill what responsibilities we do have.

And how we can rest.

The Suffering Servant King

But what will become of me? If I don't fight to make a way for myself, who will remember I'm here? How will I have a place in this world? How will I make a mark without influence? And what if I can't trust God to wield his sovereignty for my good rather than my harm?

A lack of control feels frightening in its vulnerability.

A lack of influence feels as if I might turn invisible at any moment.

I need something firm to grab on to.

So I grab on to Jesus.

In Jesus, I learn that glory and honor don't come through strength, raw power, being in control, or any sort of coercion but only through self-sacrifice, even death on a cross (Phil. 2:8). The kingdom and the cross are a package deal; we cannot have the kingdom without the sacrificial cross.

Our King, the one who sits on the throne, knows vulnerability and lack of influence. He was despised and rejected by men (Isa. 53:3). He knows the request to surrender his will (Luke 22:42). He knows the suffering that exists and manifests itself beneath his loving Father's care. He shows us that the place of honor—the most "seen" spot—belongs to the lowliest one. Jesus sits on his throne today because he gave every last piece of himself for the sake of others.

As Jesus traveled, teaching about the kingdom of God, everything he said turned the kingdom of earth on its head. In the tangible kingdom, we taste and breathe and long for titles and distinctions. But look at the lust of this, he said, pointing to the scribes and Pharisees as examples, and see how they're unwilling to be gathered by God, unwilling to submit to the control of another. They can't lose prestige and power, for this is what they use to condemn others and bestow glory on themselves.

The disciples, steeped in the earthly kingdom, expressed confusion. James and John straight out asked for power and glory from

Jesus, and Jesus warned them they didn't actually know what that meant in the kingdom.

> You know that those who are considered rulers of the Gentiles lord it over them, and their great ones exercise authority over them. But it shall not be so among you. But whoever would be great among you must be your servant, and whoever would be first among you must be slave of all. For even the Son of Man came not to be served but to serve, and to give his life as a ransom for many. (Mark 10:42–45)

The kingdom of God is populated with the meek and lowly in heart—people who don't enlist power plays or elbowing and shoving. The meek are, like Jesus, patiently long-suffering, not intent on furthering their own agenda in their own frail strength. Jesus made it clear: one day these are the people who will be given the new earth and will be invited to reign alongside him as king.

This turns us on our heads too, doesn't it?

In relation to God, he calls us children.

In relation to others, he calls us servants (Matt. 18:23).

James and John didn't know what they were asking for when they asked for power, because in the kingdom of God, power is always used to benefit the lowliest and least of these. All power is borrowed power; all influence, gifted influence. God gives us whatever power and influence we have so that we might serve. The greater the influence, the lower we must go.

Serving Our King

When my boys were small, I distinctly remember standing at the stove, stirring a pot of spaghetti sauce in preparation for dinner, with a small child clinging to my leg, and hearing the garage door open. My husband was home from work, which I was glad for, but the noise and clatter of my other boys running through the house rattled my nerves, and I still had much to do in order to get food on the table. When Kyle came in the door with a smile and arms open for welcome-home hugs, I watched as the boys ran toward him, but I myself did not go to him. I turned back to the stove and to my suddenly very important spaghetti sauce, excusing myself from warmly greeting him as a subconscious, silent protest. *Look at all that needs still to be done, and look at who is doing it!* I tried with my darting and dashing around the kitchen to manifest the old cliché before his eyes: a woman's work is never done.

The truth is that I was being stubborn. My husband and I had previously had a conversation about what we'd like to see different in our marriage. I'd asked for the feedback myself: "Are there little things that I'm not aware of that would make you feel more loved?" The only thing he'd mentioned was the moment he returned home after work. "I'd like for you to stop what you're doing for just a moment and give me a hug and kiss. That's all," he'd said. My husband rarely requests such specific changes, but I thought it was silly. Didn't he see that all I carried in a day—three young children, housework, volunteer work, part-time work, ministry, shopping, and cooking—came to a chaotic crescendo right when he returned home? Couldn't he see that I was already serving him through all of this? A hug and a kiss were frivolous and could certainly wait.

Again, the conversation. Again, the request. He didn't raise his voice (he never raises his voice). He didn't condemn (he never condemns). He again asked that I intentionally greet him at the end of the day.

Of course it was so much more for me than a simple greeting. And my response to the request said so much more about my heart than about my busy day. I didn't want to serve; I wanted to *be* served. I wanted reprieve from my day-long service. I wanted him to see me in action in order that he might validate and appreciate my service. No matter that he'd been pastoring, leading, shepherding, counseling, and managing all day. His arrival at home meant it was finally my turn to *receive*.

I know how ugly this sounds. Your heart may not be so ugly, but we all at some point are challenged by life's circumstances to serve and give not because we're looking for return but out of our love for God.

I realized that's what Kyle's request was really challenging. It was not that I didn't love my husband or want to please him. It was that I needed a deeper well of love to draw from when my emotions, will, and energy were completely dry. I needed to walk in the footsteps of Jesus, imitating his sacrificial service in honor of his Father. It didn't matter if he was feeding people or teaching. Everything he did, he did with an eye toward God the Father.

We too must consider all we do to be for God. Our service may be directed toward people and benefit them in some way, but the only way we can pour out our lives for others is if we're serving "as unto the Lord."

Greeting my husband at the door was stubbornly hard for me because I'd made it about me. But if I were to think, *This is a way I can love God (and of course my husband too)*, then the choice is clear before me.

God doesn't ask us to go without influence on this earth. He asks rather that we use whatever influence he's given us for the sake of others. We don't hoard it in order to amplify our own name; we give ourselves away to amplify his name. The world says we must climb the ladder of success. The King says we should slip our feet to lower rungs, seeking more whom we might serve.

When you are the lowest slave, no one can repay you for your kindness and generosity. Your repayment will not come from others but from above—from the One who can bestow on you what you cannot give yourself: true honor.[1]

practicing THE kingdom OF god

How can we recognize our allegiance to control and move toward our happiest allegiance: Jesus? Below are a few suggested practices, and as always, it is not the actual practice that will transform you. Ask God to speak to you and help you become wholehearted toward him.

1. Make a list of the roles or opportunities God has given you where you have power or influence. Choose one role or opportunity you've written down and decide one specific way you'll use that role or opportunity to serve someone else in the coming weeks. That service may be encouragement, meeting a need they have, or giving away your spot for their sake.

2. Make an intentional plan for how you'll practice Sabbath rest. Most of the time we think of it as going to church and not doing much else on a Sunday, but when we think of Sabbath rest we should think "different." If we work with our hands throughout the week, we can do activities that turn our minds to God and spark our affection for him. If we work with our minds throughout the week, we can choose activities that move our bodies and spark our affection for him. Whatever it is that renews our spirits, Sabbath requires intentionality and purposeful activity. How will you be intentional and purposeful in setting work aside and connecting with God this week? How can you make this a consistent practice?

3. Enact the "we" of the kingdom. Discuss with others how they practice Sabbath rest. What have they learned that can help you? What do those in your same vocation or life stage do in order to rest? What can you share with them about what you've learned?

4. We continue to discover how we are children in the kingdom of God. The next time you have opportunity to do so, observe a child interacting with his or her world and parents. What does this teach you about who you are in the kingdom of God?

5. Often what we have a tendency toward in misplaced allegiance has, at its root, a clue about how God has made us. A person tending toward control is perhaps a person who is disciplined. With properly aligned allegiance, this is a person who displays the fruits of self-control and kindness that can only come from the Holy Spirit. Ask him to grow this fruit in you. And consider: How might God, if you live submitted to him, use you and your Spirit-gifted self-control and kindness in his kingdom?

6. For further reading: 1 Timothy 6:15–16, Romans 13:1, Ephesians 1:16–23, and Mark 10:42–45.

EIGHT

escape

Becoming a mother felt to me a little like getting punched in the face. And as the great theologian Mike Tyson so wisely said, "Everyone has a plan until they get hit for the first time."[1]

My prenatal plan had been at bullet-point detail level. From the moment I saw two pink lines on the pregnancy test, I prepared to be a sleep trainer extraordinaire with a firm nap and eating schedule for the baby. You've probably already pegged me as a type A kind of gal, and you would be right. Can you also tell I prefer sleeping versus not sleeping?

Thus the punch in the face.

I kid you not that the first night we brought our little guy home from the hospital, Kyle and I announced it was bedtime to our newborn, swaddled him and placed him in the Pack 'n Play at the foot of our bed, and *fully expected* that this child understood what "lights out" meant. We climbed into bed, settled down for the night—and much to our chagrin, our little baby did not stop squeaking, wiggling, or grunting, and somehow one of the arms we'd encased like a sausage in his blanket escaped and was flopping around uncontrollably. This, of course, set off his first shrieking alarm of the night, and by night two at home, the Pack 'n Play found itself banished to the living room—still within earshot but not such *close* earshot.

I was thrilled to be a mother, but my idealistic plans were scrapped and necessitated replacing, most notably in the area of rest. I'd never been so exhausted in all my life, but it also seemed as if my mind and body were immediately alert to the slightest baby noise and would never allow me to sleep again.

The sleepless nights piled up, my nerves wore thin, and I began to understand the sage wisdom of Mike Tyson.

Once we settled into some semblance of routine, my husband tried convincing me to leave the house without the baby for an hour or two and do something for myself. The trouble was I couldn't remember what I liked to do, so I roamed the Target aisles for a while and then went to the local bookstore with its nice, plush armchairs. I didn't have the mental capacity for a whole book, so I browsed the celebrity magazines.

This quickly became my habit anytime my husband shooed me out the door: Target aisles and celebrity magazines. Celebrity magazines and Target aisles. Sometimes just Target aisles, and sometimes just celebrity magazines, and neither cost me much, if anything at all.

But it turns out they cost me a lot.

One day, after a little time away, I steered my car onto our street, saw our home, and let out a big sigh. I realized I felt more exhausted coming home than I had leaving. I'd gone out for rest and renewal in order to come home ready to reengage with my family, but I was actually returning home tired, edgy, and even a little bit annoyed that I couldn't seem to scratch that exhaustion itch. I began grumbling and pitying myself for my endless workload as a new mother, and then the thought struck me: I'd been looking for renewal in all the wrong places.

I'd been giving myself to mindless, vain things and expecting them to fill me up with life.

I'd been trying to escape and in the process had walked right into a trap.

Escape Hatches

King Escape is absolutely the ruler of this modern age, and its reign is making us something less than human. It seems to me our world has given up on ever finding hope or something worth living for, and so we go to anything or anyone that will allow us an hour or a day or even a lifetime's reprieve from dwelling on the hopelessness.

We're becoming something less than human, specifically through mindlessness—almost robotic, unconscious movement from one entertainment source to another. We're finding more and more contentment in being vacuous and empty, and we're being discipled by our cultural king of escape to be completely reactive rather than proactive and purposeful.

But sometimes escape is more than mindlessness. Sometimes we escape because we're trying to ease our own disappointment or internal conflict without actually considering what we're feeling. We're proactive in the wrong directions as an avoidance tactic. We may attempt to comfort ourselves with food, find some sort of validation through the purchase of status symbols, or establish that we're wanted through illicit sex. We simply don't want to face any negative emotions or circumstances, and so we don't. We find a way around them.

What's wrong with escape? You probably asked that question as you read about my trips to Target and to the magazine rack. We know gluttony, greed, and illicit sex are wrong, but is there anything inherently wrong with the little guilty pleasures of browsing the dollar aisle at Target or getting away from it all at the bookstore for a time? No, not necessarily.

The trouble comes, however, when we look for life where life cannot be found.

On that day when I pulled onto my street and realized how exhausted I was, for the first time I thought about what I'd been doing and why. My plan had been to take a break from being a mom by doing something—anything—that didn't involve nursing, diapering, or pushing a stroller. I wanted a little "me" time in order to do something fun, and I wanted those fun things to breathe renewal back into me. So I'd chosen to read about celebrities and their various marriages, divorces, causes, and movies.

When I stepped back to observe my choices, what had eluded me previously now seemed obvious: vanity and emptiness can't actually give peace, joy, or renewal. The people I read about were interesting people, but none of them could give me life. True soul rest and a renewed sense of purpose in my mothering would come not through mindlessness but through actually connecting my mind and heart to the source of rest and renewal: the One who made me.

The One who made me is the same One who made you, and he's made all of us *embodied* people. We have physical bodies. We were set in families—people we can see and touch. We've been located in time and space (Acts 17:26). These truths seem obvious, but they are truths we're forgetting in our rush to escape. In fact, they are becoming truths we now believe we can defy.

In his book *Amusing Ourselves to Death*, educator and cultural critic Neil Postman wrote a scathing critique of American culture's insatiable desire for entertainment. He wrote the book in 1986, long before the advent of the internet age, but his words are incredibly prophetic regarding our current day. He blames our downward spiral into mindlessness on the telegraph. Yes, the telegraph. Before the telegraph, he says, people lived locally in their communities. The big news was what happened to someone you knew across town, and one could, as a neighbor, be a part of the community's response to the day's crisis. News traveled slowly, if at all, from city to city or country to country, until Edison invented the telegraph. Suddenly, news was transported from New York City to London at the touch of a few buttons. News writers began filling their papers with reports from across the globe, making the news no longer something local with which to engage and participate in but rather *entertainment*.[2]

Does this sound familiar?

One of our acceptable forms of escape these days is, of course, the internet, specifically social media. The very existence of social media speaks truths antithetical to how God made us, because it takes us momentarily out of our physical bodies and sets our minds and hearts into other peoples' lives, many of whom we don't know.

Various dangers await us when we consistently live disembodied like this.

One, we begin to think that the people we're watching or following on social media are our friends, and in order to engage them, we give up opportunities to engage face-to-face with people physically present with us—our actual neighbors whom we're called by God to love.

Two, we begin to think the lives we see on screens should be *our* lives, leading to all sorts of jealousy, envy, comparison, and shame.

Three, we forget we're created as embodied people. We believe we can be in many places at one time, fully engaged in all of them. We believe God is asking us to carry every concern and speak about every piece of news. In other words, when we lose sight of our embodiedness, we start to believe we're godlike.

Four, we cultivate mindlessness, which grows in our lives—without us even realizing it—an apathy toward people and toward God, because mindlessness turns us inward and cultivates selfishness. We become insatiable consumers of ideas, people, and stories without having to respond in any sort of tangible way. People's lives, no matter how tragic, become our entertainment and nothing more.

So that is what's wrong with escape. When it becomes an accumulation of indulgences or an entitlement to indulge, we've walked right into the trap of a false allegiance. We're looking for life where life can't be found.

We've forgotten what real life is meant to be, because we have so many escape hatches that help us forget.

Desire, Reality, and Broken-Down Gifts

What we're really talking about here is desire. We only escape to that which we believe will quench our thirst. We reach for sustenance we think might finally quiet the hunger pains, whether the hunger is for belonging or perhaps for a sense of our world being set right.

But at some point, the game's up. We realize our thirst and hunger can go on and on without end, that the sustenance we've gobbled up has no substance to it.

There are hints of this when we're young—the Christmas present breaks even before New Year's Day, or the birthday celebration ends and normal life beckons. We bolster the letdown with thoughts of next year, or the next big thing on the calendar, or the next big toy on the horizon. We convince ourselves the next celebration will somehow be different: it won't have the letdown, it won't end, the gifts will be better, the experience will be perfect. Wisdom comes when we give consideration to the gnawing thought that we'll still have this empty feeling after next Christmas if all we think about are the toys. *There's got to be something more.*

Dissatisfaction is an excellent teacher.

Dissatisfaction teaches us that an appetite for more—desire—is actually ingrained in all of us. Our stomachs growl, touch feels good on our skin, our hearts seek happiness. We know the difference between lack and fullness, and we all prioritize fullness. We know dissatisfaction and unsettledness, and we know what it feels like to be content. Desire, in other words, is not the same as temptation, nor should we seek escape from our desires. Desire drives us to find true satisfaction, telling us our hunger and thirst surely have an end.

Dissatisfaction also teaches us that some avenues we instinctively go down in search for fullness don't actually offer what's advertised, and we should not go again on these paths. We are, however, forgetful and stubborn, so we tread grooves on the same old bare paths, thinking *this* will be the one time we finally find what we've been looking for in the place that's never offered anything but more hunger pains.

We must pay close attention to our hunger pains, letting them teach us without ruling us.

We live in a world and especially an age when we don't have to pay attention. We can immediately escape our surroundings with our phones. We can purchase things on those phones as an immediate fix for our unsettledness. We can fill and fill and fill ourselves, numbly searching for our desired fullness, but we rarely stop and think about if what we're seeking or consuming is actually satisfying us at all. We don't digest and meditate; we simply consume and move on to the next thing. It's a cotton candy kind of world.

But Jesus says that we should be on guard, paying attention to where our desires are leading us, because they *are* leading us somewhere.

For me college was a time of youthful zeal, and I remember thinking that it would always be like this—I'd never lose my sure footing in faith and neither would my friends. We'd always be on fire for Jesus, and we'd be the generation that would change the world in his name.

My college pastor, however, tempered this thought, recalling how many people he'd seen fall away from the faith in his adult years, people he'd considered solid and unwavering. I didn't want to believe him—not about myself, nor about my fellow students. Surely we'd be the exception.

And then as the years stacked up after college graduation, life got hard. Friends lost spouses to death or divorce. Children went wayward. Unemployment and mental health crises hit. I watched some, inspired, as their zeal turned into gritty, tested faith. But others fell away. They sought refuge in what they could drink, hold, or buy. Priorities shifted, and faith, in their final evaluation, seemed childish and unwarranted.

I saw then how I too could fall away, how I was walking on a narrow ledge and could so easily lose my footing if I wasn't careful. My college pastor had been right and had in fact only been echoing Jesus's own warning that there "are those who hear the word, but the cares of the world and the deceitfulness of riches and *the desires for other things* enter in and choke the word, and [the seed of the word] proves unfruitful" (Mark 4:18–19, emphasis mine).

The choking happens little by little over time as we allow our desires to rule us rather than submitting them before God. When we attempt to meet our desires outside of God, they immediately turn sour and then become the breeding ground for a host of other idolatrous sins, such as covetousness, greed, sexual immorality, and hatred. Ironically, as we pursue life where life cannot actually be found, we instead find ourselves choked out, starved, and engaged in a war for our own souls.

This is what it looks like to hold an allegiance to escape, and Jesus says we must guard against constantly escaping to wherever our desires lead us.

We all live with dissatisfaction in some form. My dissatisfaction often appears in my mind as someone else's life. *If only I had the opportunities they had; if only I had their freedom.*

Perhaps you're single and don't want to be, or maybe you wish you could move beyond living paycheck to paycheck. If only there were a spouse, if only a better job would come along, then finally life could really be lived.

And then what if the desired change becomes a reality? *Does the someone else whose life I covet have no problems at all? Does marriage end all our hungering and thirsting? Does money? If I get what I desire, is it going to fulfill me?* These are the kinds of questions I have to ask myself in order to see that I haven't outgrown my well-worn grooves;

I've simply created adult versions of them. Unless our desires find resolution in the way God designed the universe by his wisdom, they are perpetually unsatisfied.[3]

And the way God designed the universe is for us to find the fulfillment of our desires—life—in King Jesus alone.

Take Refuge

For the Christian, we know life is found in Christ, but we often continue cultivating our preferred escape hatches because we're fearful he won't actually meet our needs—that there's a bait and switch lurking somewhere up ahead. We live as if the goodness of God is only available in minuscule doses, as if his promised peace and joy are only given to a select few at the top of the spiritual food chain. In other words, we live with a scarcity mentality: we're on our own, the future is uncertain, and resources are limited, so we should get ours where we can.

According to this scarcity mentality, God is stingy and cruel, limited in capacity, and disengaged in the lives of his children. Escape teaches us so much about God, none of it true: he can't handle the reality of what we've done, the reality of our suffering, or the reality of our very real needs. And so, of course, if we believe this, we won't ever go to him as a source of life. He becomes not a refuge but rather a weak killjoy, and we run over and over to our preferred escapes to escape *him*.

This is precisely what I do, but I'm learning to remember God throughout my day and to remind myself that his resources are my resources. Scarcity doesn't exist in the kingdom of God. King Jesus stands at the ready to offer his way out when I'm tempted, his strength when I am weak, his comfort when I am hurt, and his wisdom when I don't know what to do.

Though I'm prone to run in escape to whatever resources I can muster up, what I actually need escape from is *myself* and the cultural current in which I swim. And Jesus offers that: he is my refuge and my help, and he promises to meet my needs. As we discovered in a previous chapter, he describes God as a good Father who cares well for his household, so there is always an abundance of provision for me.

That doesn't mean he will meet every desire I have. Dissatisfaction will be with us until we meet Jesus face-to-face, and this is a fact of life, perhaps even more so for the Christian, who knows of and longs for the age to come. What we do when we experience our unmet desires manifests our true allegiance. Where we run for help shows who or what we trust.

When we recognize our dissatisfaction, God invites us to escape to him for refuge. He may not meet our exact desires, but he promises to hear the cries of our hearts and transform our desires to match his, and he promises us his presence to see us through our dissatisfaction.

How do we escape to God for refuge?

It's worth repeating that we find God in his Word. In other words, we go to him and remember time and again where life is actually found. We remember we have a King, and we receive the resources he offers us.

This remembering happens as we're "good soil" (Mark 4:20) as Jesus calls it—eager receptacles for the seed of God's Word. We're "good soil" when we hear and accept the Word. There is a sense in his description of hearers bending in to catch every spoken syllable. The hearers then embrace what's been spoken by placing themselves under its authority. The Word directs the people rather than the people directing the Word.

From this way of life, the hearers grow. Gain. And then the Word multiplies in and through them.

Jesus says the fruit will be thirtyfold, sixtyfold, a hundredfold. In that time, average agricultural yields ranged from fivefold to fifteenfold, and this was considered a good crop. In Genesis 26:12, it was said that Isaac's crop was a hundredfold, and this was God's blessing on his life.

Jesus is saying here that God flourishes those who submit to him and to his Word. He will produce a great crop of fruit in them. Of love, joy, peace, patience, goodness, kindness, faithfulness, and self-control. Psalm 1 describes people like this as a tree planted by streams of water that "yields its fruit in its season, and its leaf does not wither" (v. 3). They have life. They are sturdy, strong, not easily carried away by the destructive and death-giving desires of self or the world. They are flourishing and can face the reality of life, with all its persistent dissatisfactions.

This is a promise: as we receive with a submissive heart, placing ourselves under the living Word of God, we *will* grow in faith and love and hope and joy, for this is the way the kingdom works.

A seed doesn't bear fruit overnight. In fact, it doesn't show itself at all for days, weeks, and in some cases, months. Satisfaction—true satisfaction—is something that is built over time through purposeful, intentional living. We say yes to the cares of the kingdom of God and no to the cares of this age, believing it will deliver to us *in time* what's been promised. Joy will come. Peace will increase. We will change in ways that currently are imperceptible to us but will one day seem miraculous.

This is the gain of godliness. It's the gain of living as embodied people where God has set us rather than trying to escape all the time. Instead of grabbing for more, more, more, we recognize how much we have to give, give, give. We become hungry for opportunities to reflect God's generosity by giving of ourselves, thirsty for the chance to meet the needs of others. We see the surpassing value of storing up treasure in heaven and look forward to the inheritance waiting there for us.

So, reader, do you have needs? Do you have desires? Good. Jesus says those who look in the right place, those who seek shelter under his kingship will be blessed with satisfaction (Matt. 5:6).

In your desire, instead of escaping through consumption or dis-embodied practices, reach out to Jesus. Seek refuge in him, and pour out your desires to him. Escapers consume according to the rule of their desire, but refugees receive according to their Ruler's store-houses of provision. Escapers inevitably get choked by the cares of the world, but those who seek refuge in God become healthy, strong, and fruitful.

> How precious is your steadfast love, O God!
>   The children of mankind take refuge in the shadow of
>   your wings.
> They feast on the abundance of your house,
>   and you give them drink from the river of your delights.
> For with you is the fountain of life;
>   in your light do we see light. (Ps. 36:7–9)

Holy Discontentment

There is another reason we should not try to escape: *not all restless-ness is unholy.*

Last year was one of the most disorienting I've had since the year we moved to Charlottesville from Texas with the dream in our hearts to plant a church. For ten years, I've carried that dream—nurturing it, acting on it, supporting it, and giving myself away in order to see that dream become a reality. And it has. Our church is a beautiful testament to me of God's faithfulness and goodness.

As all beautiful, living things do, the church has grown and changed over the years, but I haven't always wanted to change along with it. I've never stopped wanting the dream as it was in the begin-ning, because I've liked who I've been in it, and I've liked forging it into reality alongside my husband.

I've loved these difficult, brutal, sweet years of church planting. But we're not church planting any longer, and in all honesty, I've felt a bit lost for a while now. I've forgotten who I am apart from the dream. I, of course, am still pulsing along in the fabric of who we are as a church, but somewhere along the way, the reality of the dream became entwined with my identity.

The Lord has graciously and patiently been calling me forward to a new time and space while at the same time splitting me from these false identities I've formed for myself. With him, this invitation and splitting is *always* a call to peace and freedom. But I have hesitated time and again, holding tightly to the glorious days of the past. The disorientation and restlessness have been more real to me than God's call to freedom.

Who am I without this dream?

I am not left without dreams, however. I have a new dream forming inside, one that's incubated for several years now. My heart beats a bit faster when I imagine what might be, and I know the reality of what could be because I've sampled it already. I sense a growing passion implanted within me by God himself, but along with the passion is a catch in my spirit, a certainty that God is saying, *Not yet.* If God wills it so, this dream belongs somewhere in the future. I, however, long to reach out and grab those days and those opportunities from the future and bring them to now.

Who am I without this dream?

I am this person here, that's who I am. I'm here in this place, among these people, with this limited time and these opportunities. I am, in other words, right where God wants me to be, doing exactly what he wants me to do.

I have not liked this truth much. That is to say, I've resisted and despised the disorientation of it, of seeing one dream completed and the other far off on the horizon. In this in-between, I want to grab on to something solid, something that feels significant, something that feels like a guarantee. *I want to escape.*

But I'm not promised my dreams. I'm not promised the choice of place and opportunity. I'm promised God. And he is pointing in one direction, over and over and over: *Don't run! Simply do what is in front of you. Nothing more, nothing less.*

It's not just that I'm to do what's in front of me. It's as if he is inviting me to *enjoy* doing what's in front of me. To enjoy the smallness. Enjoy the thinking and learning and growing. Enjoy the everyday acts of faithfulness that seem insignificant. With God, there is just as much fanfare over the small and unseen as the spotlight or the stage, if it is an intentional act of faithfulness done in his honor. He is with me here in this time and space—I'm embodied, after all—and because he has me here, I'm in his will.

So what do I do with my dream? I hold it, patiently waiting, for if it is implanted by God, he won't waste the dream or the passion behind it. I also hold it *loosely*, trusting that if the dream is really just mine wrapped up in God language, he will remove it altogether. And I choose to want that if he does.

There is a tension, almost a grief, in the waiting. I feel sometimes as if I'm going backward, as if the best years are behind me or that I missed my chance. Perhaps God has moved on to someone else. Perhaps I get only one beautiful dream becoming a reality, not two.

But I know enough now to know that God doesn't waste anything. The times I've previously been limited by circumstances or graciously held back by God's providence were times of growth, almost like a seed nestled in the soil. I'd have had nothing to say, no gumption to lead in our church, if it weren't for those years of smallness. The limits and the obscurity and the lack of opportunities to use my gifts were the very things I needed in order to fulfill the purposes God had for me later.

I know he's doing the same thing in me now.

Who am I without this dream? I am his.

So I nestle myself in the soil, waiting, while he nurtures me in my holy restlessness.

practicing THE *kingdom* OF *god*

We turn now to a few suggested daily practices that God may use in your life to stop escaping him and instead turn to him for refuge and provision. Remember, it is not these actual practices that will transform you but rather the Holy Spirit who transforms you. Look for him, listen for him in Scripture, and follow his lead.

1. Study yourself and how you've lived within the past week, considering these questions: What are your escapes? Where do you consistently run when you feel dissatisfied?

2. Face your unmet desires head-on. Make a list of them. Do your escapes correspond with your unmet desires? In other words, are you attempting to meet some of your unmet desires with your escapes? What do you need to confess to God and others?

3. The next time you feel unsettled, restless, or discontent, how will you go first to Jesus and seek refuge in him?

4. Enact the body of Christ, the church. Ask several older believers how they've previously known the difference between holy and unholy dissatisfaction. How have they practically sought refuge in God in the face of their dissatisfaction?

5. Practice embodiment. Go for a walk and receive the gift from God of what you see. Spend time with someone

you love and receive the gift from God of this relationship. When a worry pops in your head, share your concern with God and receive his gift of prayer. When you lay your head on the pillow tonight, receive God's gift of sleep, as well as his gift that he continues laboring as you rest.

6. With properly aligned allegiance, we become people who display joy that can only come from the Holy Spirit. Ask him to grow this fruit of the Spirit within you. And consider: How might God, if you live submitted to him, use you and your Spirit-gifted joy in his kingdom?

7. For further reading: Matthew 5:6, Psalm 16, Psalm 46:1, Psalm 57:1, Psalm 62:8, and Psalm 121.

NINE

isolation

The sun shone bright in the kitchen the day I realized I had no one I could call. Standing at the counter, cutting a pear into bite-size pieces for my ten-month-old, I'd instead sliced my finger. I stood silent at the sink, letting water wash over the wound and watching blood swirl in the basin. After bandaging my finger, I reached down for my son, placed him in his highchair, spread the pears on his tray, and in what seemed the very next moment, woke up underneath the kitchen table. I had fainted, and it felt as if my brain was rebooting after being switched off. My body felt clammy and weak, and as I lay there, immobile, my initial panic subsided as I heard the happy gurgles of my boy, safe in his highchair, playing with his pears.

It was then that the thought intruded: *Who will I call to come help me?*

I did not have an answer, because I did not have a friend.

The knife had opened my finger, but it had opened a far greater wound, showing me the reality that I'd tried desperately to ignore, hide, and resist: I was aching with loneliness.

At that time, I was a young pastor's wife, a young mother, and young in my understanding of God's grace. When I picture myself in those years, I think of myself in two places: tucked away in my home and tangled up in my own head.

After college, I'd waited for friends to appear, just as they'd appeared in every other era of my life—through youth group and band and softball teams and housemates. Of course my activities and associations had changed, but I was still joining and doing and presenting myself where people were. But the elusive friends didn't appear, and I began to feel as if I'd forgotten how to do friendship and was no longer friend-able. In my deep insecurity, I remained isolated, both in my home and in my head.

I remember hoping another mother would invite me out after morning Bible study. I remember desiring an older pastor's wife to take me under her wing. After my pear-eating boy received a devastating diagnosis, I remember wishing others would intentionally step into my shoes and walk with me, tell me what to do, or care for me in some way.

I was lonely for a friend, but I was also like a skittish deer, overly alert regarding every action and word spoken by myself and others, quick to dart away for safe cover when I felt vulnerable.

Lonely or Isolated?

I see now that I wasn't lonely so much as I was isolated, and there is a great difference between the two. Loneliness in itself is nothing to be ashamed of. In fact, God chooses at times to call us out to the wilderness of loneliness in order to speak to us what we can only hear there. Because he always goes with us, we're never truly alone, but in those seasons when we're walking in the wilderness, knowing God alone is sustaining us can nonetheless contribute to feelings of loneliness in relation to others.

And of course, circumstances change, altering our relationships and causing loneliness. Whether we're new to a neighborhood or a church, whether a good friend has moved away or died, or whether a once close friendship has shifted, any type of change or separation can arouse a sense of loneliness and longing in our hearts.

Longing is a constant, familiar presence in relationships. When we have them, we long for those healthy relationships and happy life circumstances to remain static. When we don't have the relationships we hope for, we long for deep community and a sense of belonging. We also long for the good old days when friendships came easy and we could enjoy those friends without all the adult responsibilities and burdens mixed in.

Longing is not a misplaced desire. In fact, the longing we have for community is a *good* one. How we pursue or respond to that longing, however, is important. We must remember that perfect relationships, community, and circumstances do not exist on this side of eternity.[1] Knowing that even the best parts of life will always be imperfect helps us embrace what we do have as grace and gift, even if the current gift is aloneness with God in the wilderness. This aloneness is a gift because it teaches us to turn our desires to the Lord in prayer and swells our hearts with a hope and eagerness for our true home with Jesus.

But isolation is wholly different from loneliness.

Isolation is an intentional choice: it's the closed door, the wall built, the sealed off heart. Isolation is choosing self-protection over connection, reconciliation, and vulnerability.

I was lonely in those years precisely because I was isolated—my choices had formed me. *I* was the reason for my loneliness.

As I look back at who I was, I see a lonely girl with a stubborn misconception of how the Godward life works. I see a girl who was lonely *because* of her stubborn misconception. I was looking for the perfect best friend and the perfect church community and the perfect friend group. At the same time, however, I was afraid to ask for help, afraid to initiate, afraid to ask about what I didn't know, and deathly afraid of allowing others to see my insecurities and uncertainties. I, of course, couldn't have voiced any of this. All

I knew is that I didn't want to be lonely but I wanted others to do all the work of breaking into my isolation. And I wondered bitterly why God wasn't giving me the gift of community I read about in Scripture.

I stopped praying about it somewhere along the way, but I kept on crying tears tinged with blame.

And all throughout that time, with each tear that fell, God was answering the prayers I'd long ago stopped praying. He was good to me in my aloneness; he was the friend who was constantly present, and he was patient with my immaturity and misconceptions. But he was also answering with real people, *imperfect* people (like me), who lived beside me and went to church with me and who were a few steps ahead and behind me. I see this now, but at the time I couldn't see past my standards and all of my bitter longings. If I'd just looked around with Spirit-filled eyes, and if I'd just been willing to take a few risks of vulnerability and initiation, I would have experienced the answer God was trying to give me.

That's what I learned that day when the knife cut my finger and opened my heart. It wasn't that I didn't have anyone I could call; it was that I was *afraid* to call.

My allegiance was to self-protection above all else.

Isolation was my fortress.

What Happens in the Dark Gets Distorted in the Dark

Why would we choose to bow to King Isolation when we hate the feeling of loneliness that often comes with it?

It's simple: isolation feels safe. If we don't interact on an emotional or spiritual level with others, we believe we won't get hurt as we have in the past. We can hide, nursing old wounds or keeping our shame and pet sins secret. In isolation, we're never forced to change, grow, forgive, or confess. We don't have to worry about becoming a burden to anyone or about carrying the messy, cumbersome burdens of others. If we build figurative walls between others and ourselves, it feels as if we're protected.

However, isolation's promise of warmth and safety delivers something else entirely: it cuts off the oxygen and light we need in order to live and grow and be human in the way God designed us to be. Unchecked isolation eventually shuts us in utter darkness.

And distortion grows in the dark.

The worst nights of sleep I get are when my husband is out of town. I usually stay up too late, and when I finally determine it's bedtime, I start my rounds.

I check the locks.

I turn on the outside floodlights.

Before heading upstairs to our bedroom, I flip on the hall light before turning off the final light downstairs. The hall light has another switch right outside my bedroom door, so I have a light on until I'm within reach of my room.

The worst part of the night is turning off my bedside lamp—the last light gone. In the darkness, I am instantly alert to every out-of-place noise, and my mind instantly recalls every scary *Dateline* episode I've ever seen.

As my mind churns, I create a plan for how I'll get away from whatever intruder is sure to come, how I'll rescue my children from their rooms, and where we'll go for safety once we're outside in the cold, dark night. I try to convince myself to think of other things, and just as I'm drifting off to sleep, the house creaks, and I'm wide awake again.

Thoughts and fears get distorted in the dark. Small noises I otherwise wouldn't notice if my husband were next to me become factual evidence in my mind of the presence of a serial killer. One thought of what *could be* becomes an entire scenario that I'm convinced *will* occur.

This is exactly what happens to us in the darkness of spiritual isolation. Thoughts, fears, and desires become distorted and disproportionately larger than what's real and true and good. On high alert, we're swept away by what we feel or by whatever thought happens to pass through our minds. In turn, we become highly susceptible to lies about God, others, and ourselves. Because we're the only one in the figurative room, our preferences, needs, and desires become ultimate. We begin to worship ourselves, cultivating the flesh, following in action wherever our thoughts and desires take us.

For instance, as an introvert, I'm tempted to allow this aspect of my personality to define me and be the scaffolding on which I build my life. What I mean by "define me" is that I'm tempted to follow my instincts into total isolation, elevating my personality type above the commands of God. In isolation, how I want things becomes my top priority, and I'm annoyed when even my own family members enter and disturb my quiet sanctuary.

I am instead defined as a person found "in Christ," filled and empowered by the Spirit of Christ to lay my life down for others. To focus on my personality type, although given to me by God, is to set my mind on the flesh—myself (Rom. 8:6).

Any thought, desire, or drive that elevates self and diminishes the Spirit should set off alarm bells in our head. God gives us our personalities not for our own pleasure but for our service to him.

It's difficult to know and remember this, however, when we're only ever intimately interacting in a real way with ourselves.

The Tentacles of Shame

The primary thoughts that distort and grow in the darkness of isolation are shame and blame.

No wonder we hide, because these are some of the most vulnerable, intimate, pain-ridden thoughts and experiences we could have.

Shame is a feeling of humiliation or distress caused by the consciousness of wrong or foolish behavior.[2] In other words, we've sinned, we know we've done wrong, and we feel badly about having done so. If we don't know where to put our shame or how to diffuse it, we tuck it away, hoping no one will ever know what we've done.

Unfortunately, shame has tentacles. Shame stemming from real sin that has not been forced out of isolation quickly compounds. Shame can even grow out of sin we've confessed before God and received forgiveness for—the thought that others may not respond with the same mercy and grace can keep us in prolonged isolation.

For example, perhaps a Christian woman has continually used pornography but has confessed and repented of her sin to God. It's good that she's done so, but because she often hears pornography discussed as a "man's issue," she's been afraid to confess her sin to others and bring others in as ongoing accountability. As she's continued carrying this alone, shame over what she's already confessed and repented of—sin that Jesus has forgiven—has crept into her life. This is false shame, a distortion that's grown in the dark. God has removed her sin as far as the east is from the west, and he thinks of it no more. But the enemy, the father of lies, has convinced her of exactly the opposite and works to keep her quiet and isolated.

There is a reason the Bible tells us to confess our sins to one another (James 5:16). Confession is an invitation for the light of God's love, truth, and grace to be voiced to the person confessing. We often stay in our monologues, convincing ourselves the distortions are true, when in fact we need a dialogue with fellow believers who remind us of what Christ has done for us.

The woman repenting of her pornography use would be greatly helped by conversation and accountability in order to experience the full extent of God's healing.

Think of all the ways our private thoughts morph and terrorize us: comparison, envy, guilt, doubt, and more. How do we often respond to these? We hold them close, hoping no one will see. We carry the weight of our sin on our own, afraid to tell what's in our heart. In this secrecy, shame takes root. *God can't forgive me. God can't use me. God's not for me. Perhaps I'm on my own. Perhaps I'm unwanted. If I tell this, what will they think?*

The Acidic Bitterness of Blame

Shame grows in the dark, but so does blame. Whereas shame stems from our sin, blame stems from the sins of others against us.

When we've been hurt, we tend to isolate self-protectively, and in our isolation, like car mirrors, our wounds appear larger and more vicious than they actually are. I'm not saying they don't hurt or that the process of forgiveness is easy, but rather that in isolation we tend to nurse and rehearse our wounds until they seem altogether unforgivable. Just as unspoken shame leads to distorted, false shame, unspoken hurt compounds and leads to distorted, false hurt.

Since we're the sovereigns in our isolation, we become the ultimate judge, and in our supremacy we get to determine what their appropriate punishment should be. We put words in their mouth and motives in their heart, and we have the same conversations with them in our heads on repeat. This false hurt is the self-inflicted hurt of bitterness and mercilessness, and both become our sin against God—the sinned-against becomes the sinner.

There is a reason the Bible tells us to go to one another and deal openly with hurts. Confronting in love and being confronted in love enable us to see the reality of who we are and what we're capable of, and help us to turn toward God for help in order to change. Confrontation helps us see and experience the magnitude of God's grace and power and keep hardness of heart at bay.

Confession and repentance are incredible gifts within the kingdom of God, but we love our isolation too much to partake of them. We like to think we don't need anyone but ourselves, although our lonely ache and the nagging feeling that we're missing something relationally tell us otherwise.

Self-reliance is a feeding of the flesh, and the flesh is death.

We may be lulled by the lie of safety and comfort in self-reliance, but in fact we're on a pathway to stunted growth and pain.

We, Not Me

Isolation is antithetical to the kingdom of God.

As the disciple Peter followed along behind Jesus, he heard Jesus's response to a rich man who questioned how he could enter the kingdom of God. Jesus drew the same line he draws for each of us: entrance comes only through him. After the rich man walked away from Jesus, still trying to ease his hunger with possessions, Peter, forever the teacher's pet, raises his hand and says to Jesus, "See, we have left everything and followed you" (Mark 10:28).

Peter certainly contrasts the rich man. The rich man walked away from true life in order to cling to his own self-made kingdom of possessions and wealth, thinking he might find life in something that is lifeless. Peter, on the other hand, left his former life, even his livelihood, to follow after Jesus. Speaking for all the disciples, he says, "Where else could we go? You have the words of eternal life!" (see John 6:68).

Peter shows us a picture of our own Christianity. We've let go of all our safety nets, all our plan Bs, all our potential self-oriented kingdoms and have clung tightly to Jesus. There's been loss in order to have gain.

Jesus said there is in fact a reward for those seeking the rule and reign of Jesus:

> Truly, I say to you, there is no one who has left house or brothers or sisters or mother or father or children or lands, for my sake and for the gospel, who will not receive a hundredfold *now in this time*, houses and brothers and sisters and mothers and children and lands, with persecutions, and in the age to come eternal life. (Mark 10:29–30, emphasis mine)

What is the reward?

The one becomes a hundred. The individual becomes many.

The reward is our brothers and sisters who also seek refuge beneath the King's rule—the church.

This is a *kingdom*, after all, and a kingdom implies many citizens.

We are, together, a "chosen race, a royal priesthood, a holy nation, a people for his own possession. . . . Once [we] were not a people, but now [we] are God's people" (1 Pet. 2:9–10).

In the Old Testament, the Israelites possessed the kingdom of God. God's redemptive activity in history had been channeled through the nation of Israel, and the blessings of the divine rule had been bestowed upon his people. Gentiles could share these blessings only by entering into relationship with Israel.[3] But the Israelites rejected the kingdom as manifested in Jesus, and therefore Jesus gave his kingdom to the church.

Now, in this time, the church is the ruled kingdom. In many ways, the kingdom of God is mysterious and as unseen as a seed planted in the ground, but one way we can know, see, touch, and interact with the kingdom of God is by gathering together with and living among our brothers and sisters in the church. The Spirit of Christ calls us together, unites us in love, and gifts us to serve one another. The church is the King's power over the King's people with the King's presence and precepts.[4]

In other words, the church is a foretaste of the coming of the consummated kingdom.

Did you notice that Jesus says that when the gospel costs us, and when we face persecutions in this present time, the church is our reward? We lose—we're subtracted from—but then we gain.

We often think of persecution as facing martyrdom for our faith, but the daily persecution we all face is the stabbing pain of saying no to our flesh as it tries to drag our allegiance away from Christ.

Gazing at Jesus on the cross, remembering his claim on us, acts as a knife, continuously and persistently cutting away all other idolatrous loves. The cross pursues us and crucifies all of our claims to self-rule or self-glory, and this can be excruciatingly painful.

But Jesus said that when we leave all to follow him—when we set Christ as King in our hearts above possessions and family and marriage and vocation and power and personality—we actually are enveloped into a corporate follow-ship fighting with and beside us in our own battle against temptation and sin.

A perfect example of this is Jesus on the cross (the ultimate cost of submission to his Father), saying to his mother as John stood nearby, "Woman, here is your son," and to John, "Here is your mother" (see John 19:26–27). Jesus says to them, in their grief and suffering over his unjust death, "I don't leave you alone. You have each other."

Through the cost and the grief comes the reward of relationships.

This is where we hear the record screeching to a stop. *Wait, what? The church is my reward? These people who imperfectly love, imperfectly serve, imperfectly forgive, and imperfectly know me?*

The church doesn't always feel like a reward, so why would Jesus say it's so?

The church is a foretaste of heaven, a family of brothers and sisters gathered around Christ as Lord. But they are also help along the way as we move toward the consummated kingdom. We are to encourage one another and aid one another through this life. We can learn from others' modeling of the gospel, and they from us. They can bear our grief and celebrate our joys, and we can do the same for them. The point of the church isn't to make us happy and meet all of our needs. The point is that we seek first the kingdom together. I'll seek the rule and reign of Jesus for you, and you for me.

Think about where I went when I recognized my envy: I went to a sister. I not only needed to confess my sin to her but also needed her going forward to help me not succumb to the spiral of death.

Hearing her express God's forgiveness was like hearing God say it to me himself. She was the church to me in that moment.

Confession and repentance before King Jesus bring us back to life, and our brothers and sisters nurture that life in ongoing ways.

However, when we struggle with sin, shame, or blame, this is often the very time we move *away* from everyone and everything that helps reinforce the gospel in our lives. Our greatest temptation toward isolation comes when we most need the church surrounding us.

The enemy's strategy to tempt us toward isolation is actually a common military tactic used in war. If you can separate your opponent from their supply lines—reinforcements of people, supplies of food and ammunition—it's just a matter of attrition and time before they're defeated.

Our enemy doesn't fight fair in the war for our heart's allegiance.

In our shame, we hear whispers in our head of sin, the flesh, and evil that say, *No one is as bad as you. You're the only one who deals with this. If people knew this about you, they would reject you.* When our response to these whispers is to run into isolation, we are devoured by the world and our enemy.

In our blame, we hear whispers that fuel our own sin and flesh: *You are a victim. You're entitled to your anger. You don't have to forgive. You'll never have joy again because of what that person did to you.* We run into self-protective isolation and, likewise, get devoured by our own bitterness.

God has given us grace upon grace in the form of his people. We *will not* grow and change into Christlikeness unless and until we engage with his people for mutual growth. We will instead become distorted Christians as we choose to continue in the darkness of isolation.

The call, then, is to step into the light and link arms with our brothers and sisters.

Let us say, "Thy kingdom come," together.

Partake of the Kingdom Now in This Time

According to Charles Spurgeon, "As soon as a man has found Christ, he begins to find others."[5]

This pursuit of relationships must characterize our lives.

In order to make this pursuit our heartbeat, we must know that the church is "the manifold wisdom of God" (Eph. 3:10). We will come to know and understand the love of Christ through the love of others, and we will understand the extent of Christ's love and sacrifice when we love others in return. God, in his beautiful wisdom, has designed it to be this way; therefore, our individual faith cannot be separated from the corporate kingdom of God. In fact, our corporate life together with other Christians is where heaven meets earth, for the kingdom of God is present where men and women have subjected themselves to King Jesus.

The kingdom of God comes tangentially alive between you and me.

So it is not just for our own sake that we seek community. If we approach the church with our preferences, needs, and desires at the forefront, this is once again a cultivation of the kingdom of self.

We seek *mutual* community, both for our sake and for the sake of others, and so that the kingdom of God can be seen and experienced by outsiders. The love between us is their standing invitation to come in and receive.

So we bring ourselves to the church as an offering.

My story is for you. The comfort Christ has given me is for you (2 Cor. 1:6). My gifts are for you. My service is for you. My experiences are for you. My hard-won lessons are for you. And all of these that you have are for me. I need you, and you need me. God nurtures and forms us through one another.

I like to consider the culture of a place. How did San Francisco become San Francisco and New York City become New York City?

Why is the town I grew up in different from the one where I currently live, and how did they each take on the personality they have? What influences have quietly been at play? What historical decisions or community concerns made it what it is?

It wasn't an individual that formed my city; it was formed by people interacting and responding to one another. What concerned one person became the concern of their neighbors; what failed to cause alarm in individuals together cultivated systemic problems.

Likewise, the kingdom of God is a corporate body made of many parts. If we are isolated, holding back, afraid of difficulty or messiness, or simply apathetic to the needs and concerns of others, we are hindering others and ourselves from Christlikeness. Keeping our false allegiances alive only keeps us busy maintaining our emptiness.

Friends, if we're doing community right, we're going to get hurt and hurt others. But God has made provisions for this messy thing he calls his church: he's given us the gifts of confession, repentance, and forgiveness. He's made these foundational commands as we bear with one another in love and continue cultivating the kingdom together.

In order to partake of the manifold wisdom of God, we must resist isolation and be willing to engage the most difficult parts of relationships with our brothers and sisters. When Jesus said, "In this world you will have trouble" (John 16:33 NIV), he didn't exclude his church. Most of Paul's letters, in fact, address conflict and disunity in churches, so we shouldn't expect our relationships to be obstacle-free. If God has given us the ministry of reconciliation and the gifts of confession and repentance, certainly he expects we'll have to regularly enact those gifts.

Isolation is not an option for the child of God (Prov. 18:1).

In order to resist an allegiance to selfish isolation, we must remember the rest of John 16:33: "In this world you will have trouble. *But take heart! I have overcome the world*" (NIV, emphasis mine).

This is why we must cling to the anchor of Christ's perfect love. The wounds still hurt but they don't rock our identity or our security. We have a God who lives within us and helps us say and receive hard words, who helps us navigate conflict and wounds, and who teaches us how to reconcile and forgive. With our hope in him and our hope that we will one day watch with our own eyes as he overcomes the world and all its imperfections, we can embrace the messiness of community.

And we can see the manifold wisdom of God on display.

practicing THE kingdom OF god

Below I've suggested some daily practices God may use to pull you out of your self-imposed isolation and toward his church. Remember, it is not the actual practice that will transform you but rather the Holy Spirit who transforms you. Look for him, listen for him in Scripture, and follow his lead.

1. In what ways are you tempted to isolate?

2. Do you have lingering hurt that is keeping you from partaking of God's gift to you—the church? How will you deal with that hurt in a way that resists isolation?

3. Have you ever shared something you felt shame about with another person? How did God use that confession in your life? Has anyone ever shared something with you

they felt shame about? How did God use that confession in your own life?

4. Most chapters of the book so far have held concluding practices requesting you enact the "we" of the kingdom. In any of your responses so far, have you actually gone to a trusted friend, mentor, or pastor in order to confess or repent of a false allegiance? Why or why not? What often keeps you from bringing others into your questions, doubts, or sin struggles?

5. Enact the "we" of the kingdom: share one or two things that God is doing in your life with a trusted friend this week. Ask them what God is doing in their lives and commit to praying for them.

6. For further reading: 1 John 1:5–10, Ephesians 3:10–13, 2 Corinthians 1:3–7, Romans 12, Hebrews 12:1, and James 5:16.

TEN

approval

I attended a large church during my college years that was filled to the rafters with students. The college ministry, therefore, was robust and allowed for each of us to find unique areas of service and ministry. We brought the energy and zeal, and the leadership simply turned us loose; it was all very formative and exciting.

I myself joined the drama team.

I'd never in my life acted, I had a terrible singing voice, and I was terrified of appearing foolish in front of hundreds of my peers, but this, I still somehow determined, was my calling.

A team of misfits, we met up each Wednesday night and, thinking ourselves incredibly clever, sat around in a corner of the church and created skits out of thin air, cracking ourselves up in the process.

One of the older guys was our Designated Messiah. No matter the skit, he'd inevitably find himself standing on a chair, arms stretched out as if on a cross, and head hanging in indication of death.

I usually played the ditzy parts, a foil to the straight-laced, earnest college student seeking spiritual truth.

(We thought we were hilarious, but my college boyfriend, who later became my husband, endlessly ribbed me, nicknaming our drama team "Dramamine" after the medication that makes one instantly drowsy.)

There was one skit, however, in which I didn't play the ditzy part. I was given the dramatic role, probably because I was the only one who could produce tears on cue. (My teenage years came in handy after all.) I played a girl who approached different people in succession, holding a rose out to them with a pleading look in my eye. Each person would put their arm around me and pretend to love me, but then would take a few petals off my rose and throw them down, a show of rejection and abandonment. I'd go on to the next person, hoping for a different response, pleading with more and more urgency, but never finding the acceptance I craved. Finally, I'd take center stage with only a bare stem, face the audience, and the tears would roll.

We performed this skit many times for various audiences, and the tears came right on cue every single time.

Apparently I resonated with the character and her situation more than I cared to admit, even to myself.

Wanting to Be Wanted

If there's one thing I'd change about my high school and college years—aside from my hair and fashion sense, of course—it's the number of boys I dated. I was obsessed with boys, with having a boyfriend, and most of all with wondering what boys thought of me, so I sometimes dated boys just because they showed interest in me and not because I was all that interested in them. Their interest was a spark inside of me, an electric neon sign flickering on that said, "I'm wanted."

When I wasn't dating anyone, I lay in bed at night, fantasizing myself to sleep, imagining scenarios where the boy I liked at the moment asked me out and what romantic date we'd go on together. I'd combine my first name with his last, and see what it sounded like rolling off the tongue, all the while imagining what sort of man I'd eventually marry. I hoped for the romantic comedy kind of ending with a handsome boy who would be as obsessed with me as I was with him. I wanted that neon sign on forever.

I never considered that the romantic comedies I watched always ended just at the moment the actual relationship began. The obstacles and misunderstandings that kept the two lovebirds apart would finally be overcome and then all else, it was assumed by the happy ending, would be smooth sailing. The woman was completed by the man and the man by the woman, and romantic love as the desired end had been found. Done.

Sigh.

As I lay in my bed, considering my own desired end, I remember thinking that the struggles I had with temptation in my thought life regarding boys would finally be over when I said *I do*. Their ability to turn that neon sign off or on inside of me would finally end. I wouldn't struggle any longer with confidence, physical appearance, body image, or sexual temptation. The obstacles and misunderstandings that tripped me up inside, keeping me from fulfillment, would finally be overcome.

I did meet a handsome boy, and he was different from all the others. I felt with him as if I were riding a train propelled by something other than me, something other than him, something other than just physical attraction—something I knew in my spirit to be God himself. God compelled me toward Kyle with such clarity and peace that when he asked if I'd marry him, I said yes without hesitation.

Aside from my decision to follow Jesus, it's been the best decision I've ever made.

I was surprised to find, however, that real life begins precisely where the romantic comedies conclude. I became a married woman, and much changed—my address, sleeping arrangement, name, towels and dishes, and jewelry—but my mind didn't. The grooves of thought I'd cultivated, the way of daydreaming myself to sleep, the neon sign I'd set front and center in my heart—surprisingly, those came with me into my marriage.

As a married woman, I still noticed that other men were attractive. I still wanted to be thought of as attractive by men other than my husband. I even struggled with the idea of never again experiencing the thrill of a new dating relationship, when the neon sign would flicker on and send a little jolt through my insides. I was surprised by these same old mental temptations, because I'd always believed that an open and right avenue for physical and sexual intimacy (marriage) would instantly negate temptation's power in my life.

At first, I assumed this unforeseen temptation meant something was wrong with me. No Christian woman had ever warned me of it, so I was ashamed at being the "only one" facing such thoughts. Soon after, however, a godly friend confessed to me that she was thinking of a male coworker too much because she enjoyed his attention, and I realized with some relief how "no temptation has overtaken [me] that is not common to man" (1 Cor. 10:13).

I wasn't the only one with temptation whispering in my mind, but I also knew I needed to be constantly on guard and take every thought captive in order to honor my husband and honor the Lord. I needed to cultivate new grooves of thought in my mind.

I began by considering *why* I was tempted in these specific ways. The answer: I'd brought my idols into marriage and set them up beside all the Lenox china we'd registered for and received as gifts. I desired to be found attractive and to experience the thrill of new love, because these labels—Beautiful, Desirable, Pursued—had always proven to me that I was wanted. *I craved a certain kind of approval.*

I'd never considered these as false allegiances. After all, loving and being loved are good things. Beauty is a gift from God. Relationships are as well.

But now that fleeting romantic love had morphed into steady, faithful love, and I could no longer feel the neon sign flickering on after being off, I saw how these allegiances had moved beyond good and become something ultimate that I'd bowed down to and worshiped. I'd never really known what sacrificial love, true beauty, and godly relationships were, and in honor of the husband I truly loved and the God who loved me, I committed to finding out.

In order to know, I'd need to live as I'd vowed to live, renouncing all other loves, all other desires, all other desires of being desired, all other allegiances. It was ultimately a choice of what to do with my thoughts, because this choice would direct and form and inform my desires. And I act upon my desires.

Seeking Approval through Validation

This is a picture of what it's like to become a Christian. We commit to loving Jesus alone and having no other loves before him, but we face the ongoing challenge of keeping good things—good things God himself has given—from becoming ultimate in our lives and usurping Christ's place. Sometimes we even set out in pursuit of those good things in the name of Christ, but deep down we're simply using him as a cloak for our selfish ambition.

Such is the case with love.

Love and acceptance are good gifts, but they can easily morph into a false allegiance if we're not careful. In fact, we face the most temptation when God has clearly implanted a *good* desire in us but we currently have no outlet to act on that desire. Perhaps it's sexual desire as a single, or it's experiencing infertility within marriage when children are desired, or it's a desire to use skills and gifts but having no current opportunities. Often our response is to seek what will meet our desires, whether through relationships, roles, or responses from others. These culminate in the labels we give ourselves or *hope* to give ourselves—a form of approval called validation—and we view life through the lens of these labels.

Our social media bios tell this story: Spouse. Parent. Pastor.

Our small talk: "What do you do?" Architect. Teacher. Engineer. Student.

The letters by our names: Mrs. MD. PhD.

The pictures we share: Best friends. Trips. Happy families. Fit bodies.

We hope people see that we're wanted, intelligent, included, adventurous, healthy, accomplished, hardworking, and creative.

All of these are good things; anything we have been given or have accomplished or enjoy are gifts of grace, every single one.

But what if we don't have a label that we desperately want? What if we've had a label we loved and it got stripped away? What if we have a label we don't want and actually despise? We tend to believe our worth is wrapped up in certain labels.

We all face this predicament at one time or another—some of us through circumstances that will never change in this life—and these are the exact places in our hearts where our allegiance to King Jesus gets tested most. The longing and at times despair we feel in an unmet desire can so easily turn to feelings of emptiness, worthlessness, invisibility, shame, frustration, and bitterness. These feelings often become a label unto themselves, which we wear like name tags only we ourselves see.

I know what it's like to desperately desire a label and also desperately desire to *rid* myself of a label.

For the longest time, I wanted to be a published author. I spent years writing in obscurity, mostly for myself. When I began to tell others about my secret hobby, I felt as if I were standing before them completely naked, requesting a raw critique. Although publication seemed so far out of reach, time spent writing only fed the desire more. I wanted to write words that others would see, and I wanted those words to give voice to others' experiences in a helpful way.

And then someone took a chance on me. A book would sit in the bookstore with my name on the cover! When I signed the contract, I couldn't imagine what the book's release day would feel like, but as I proudly strapped on the label of "author"—one I'd desired so long—I felt like a firework bursting into a million shards of color. I'd finally arrived.

The book came out, and then another, and then another. I'm thankful for the privilege of writing, and I will do it as long as I have opportunity, but there were obstacles and difficulties in this work I never saw coming. As soon as the ink dried on that first contract and my heart firework dissipated, my goal line moved, the panic set in, and the hard work began. The book came out, and shockingly it wasn't a *New York Times* bestseller. Some people in my life celebrated, and some yawned. Strangers wrote reviews on the internet, and I was once again standing naked, but this time before the world. Or at least the very small world that knew the book existed.

When I say I know what it's like to desperately desire a label and also to desperately desire to rid myself of a label, sometimes those have been different labels—but sometimes they are one and the same. Every label comes as a rose cut from the bush. There is beauty in difficult, unwanted things, and there are thorns that come with good things—relationships, community, children, marriage, church, and vocation, to name a few. These good things become painful at times for many reasons, but I'm starting to see how my *idealism* of what's good creates pain for me. When I expect good things to give me ultimate joy, and when I expect they can (and should) be perfect, I don't equate the challenges that inevitably come in them with God's goodness and growth in me. Idealism in any area can easily become idolatry: trying to force perfection from the created rather than turning to see the perfection of my Creator.

When we demand perfection from life, we make our desired labels the most defining aspect of who we are, and we're unable to receive gifts as gifts.

To idealize is to idolize.

When we realize this, we don't have to then become hopeless, as if the good cannot actually be good. Instead, we see that who we are and everything we have is a gift from God, and we're free to enjoy and use those gifts as an offering back to him. This is life.

We often believe the opposite: it's only when we get what we desire or we rid ourselves of what we don't desire that we'll finally experience life. We'll be at peace, happy, and self-assured. But there's always another finish line, another accolade to reach for, another person who's doing it better than us. And getting that label, whatever it is, comes with its thorns. No one has achieved or married or parented or exercised their way out of the thorns, and no one ever will.

Our souls simply weren't made for labels. Our souls weren't made for fame, or millions of dollars to spend on ourselves, or human relationships as our ultimate end. *Life is not found in labels.*

Many people across time have tried telling us this.

Solomon, who tried on for size every possible human label, summarized his pursuits this way: "I have seen everything that is done under the sun, and behold, all is vanity and a striving after wind" (Eccles. 1:14). "Everything . . . done under the sun" is another way of saying that we look for life in manmade thought and attainment and can't ever grasp it—because it's not there.

Celebrities have unknowingly echoed Solomon's wisdom. After winning three Super Bowl rings, Patriots quarterback Tom Brady said in an interview some years ago:

> Why do I have three Super Bowl rings, and still think there's something greater out there for me? I mean, maybe a lot of people would say, "Hey man, this is what it is." I reached my goal, my dream, my

life. Me, I think: God, it's got to be more than this. I mean this can't be what it's all cracked up to be. I mean, I've done it. I'm 27. And what else is there for me?[1]

We just don't want to believe them. We laugh and say, "Oh, that must be so hard." We think if we were to achieve our desired labels, somehow we'd be the exception to the sense of vanity Solomon warned of or the sense of emptiness Tom Brady voiced.

I'll say it again: our souls weren't made for this—not for self-focus, self-glorification, or self-satisfaction.

Our souls were made to use everything we have, given or acquired, rose or thorn, to showcase the importance and beauty of God. Every relationship, every role, every present moment is how God has determined we can best know him and make him known.

Solomon discovered this in the end, when he'd gained and lost and been around the block a time or two. He said, "The end of the matter. . . . Fear God and keep his commandments, for this is the whole duty of man" (12:13).

This is an available opportunity for everyone, no matter who they are.

An Allegiance of Pleading Eyes

Will work for love.

That might as well be my life motto; I've adhered to it so closely. Instead of a beautiful red rose, I've held this cardboard sign like a beggar beside every decent and acceptable avenue I've been able to find.

I'll sign up for that thing you want me to do, sure, even though I don't have space in my calendar for it and despite the fact that fulfilling this obligation will lead to stress I'll inevitably take out on my kids.

I'll bend myself to your will for my life, sure, because I dare not feel the sting of having disappointed your expectations.

I'll take on this ministry opportunity, sure, because you'll see what I can do and you'll marvel, and I'll know my great worth in your eyes.

I'll anticipate your desires, sure, and mold myself according to them.

I'll do whatever it takes, if it means you won't leave me behind or shove me aside.

Whether we seek respect, admiration, inclusion, a sense of validation, or even self-approval, it's dramatic and touching when it happens in a skit on the stage, but it's ugly and downright painful in real life.

This is what allegiance to King Approval looks and feels like. It's an allegiance characterized by pleading eyes—we turn them wherever we think we'll find value and worth. These are the eyes of the girl holding out the rose to the boy she likes or to the social circle she longs to be included in or to the boss in the corner office.

We'll do anything to be loved.

Often our pleading eyes lock onto one person in particular, perhaps most often the one we sense is withholding their approval. This is the person who holds the gavel, the ruler, or the level, and we plead with them to find us favorable. They hold sway over our lives in ways we struggle to even recognize.

'When approval is king, everyone's eyes are on another, taking what we want from fellow beggars but calling it what we need. We pass around our pittances, and we're never far from starving.

We've come by this allegiance honestly. We are, as C. S. Lewis calls us, Sons of Adam and Daughters of Eve, who "exchanged the truth about God for a lie and worshiped and served the creature rather than the Creator" (Rom. 1:25).

Adam and Eve passed down genetic spiritual blindness through their sin, eyes that remain aware in our darkness of the judgments of other people but are unaware of and disinterested in the judgments of God. What also remains is a God-given desire for love and belonging, so naturally we marry that desire with people. God *does* gift us love and belonging in communion with others, but the conclusive judgment of our ultimate worth as human beings doesn't come from anyone *but* him.

There are grave consequences when we give allegiance to approval.

This allegiance, as they all do, gives to its subjects. There is the pittance, after all. But the pittance doesn't last. There must be a constant seeking, working, and begging—an insatiable craving for more. The one who bows to approval cannot actually grasp it. No word of affirmation or encouragement can truly be received, even when it comes as directed by God through others, because we must immediately set out in search of the next word that will let us know once and for all we're truly accepted and loved.

At the same time, our allegiance to approval makes us overly sensitive, self-protective, and closed off to true intimacy in relationships. Approval acts ironically—the very act of seeking security in relationships with others breaks them apart. The very act of trying to grab love causes it to move out of reach. The very thing we think will help and settle our relationships with others actually hurts us and those we bow before, because people become objects for our fulfillment, a means to an end.

But there is a greater consequence than all others, one I quake to think of.

Imagine if my husband Kyle were to bring me a dozen roses on a date night, hold them before me, fall to his knees in emphatic declaration of love, recite an original sonnet—and the whole while have his eyes on the beautiful brunette sitting next to us. That date is not going to end well, but more importantly, it would be a sign of something disastrously wrong in our relationship.

Where the eyes look matters, specifically the spiritual eyes of the heart.

When we look to other people for our approval, we fail to see God. And when we fail to see God, we miss receiving the love we're desperately searching for.

You Have His Allegiance

The fact of the matter is that some people will *demand* our allegiance to their approval through manipulation or by taking our emotions ransom. Whether in a middle school cafeteria or in an extended family, some are "in" and some are "out," sometimes in a physical sense and sometimes in an emotional sense.

There have always been gatekeepers, people who set themselves up as judge and jury, meting out bits of approval as those around them act according to their expectations.

Such was the case even for Jesus.

Jesus was maligned by most and truly loved by a few. Throughout his life, he faced relentless questioning, verbal attacks, misrepresentation, and slander by the religious gatekeepers—the Pharisees and Sadducees. His own people. He came declaring the kingdom, and he was rejected as a spokesperson from God.

The crowds would eventually leave him, and his friends would as well. When he went to his death, he went as a solitary figure, his cross carried by a man who had never heard his name.

What does this tell us? Being rejected or disapproved of doesn't weigh in when it comes to measuring our worth before God. Being disapproved of by others is not a sin.

But *seeking* their approval is.

So we must go to war against the allegiance of approval. The way we do this is to follow in the steps of Jesus the King.

When the spiritual gatekeeper of the kingdom of earth, Satan himself, appeared before Jesus and offered his approval, given Jesus's fulfillment of certain nefarious expectations, Jesus looked at his Father (Matt. 4:1–11).

Satan laid out his first requirement: *Turn these stones to bread and demonstrate your true worth.*

Jesus looked at his Father.

Throw yourself off the temple and demonstrate your true power.

Jesus looked at his Father.

Bow down and worship the prince of this world and earn true glory.

Jesus looked at his Father.

Jesus refused to engage. He didn't play the approval game. His tactic was to set his eyes on God, because he knew that God saw him, and that God's pleasure in him was full. Jesus lived with the approval of God in mind. He already had his Father's approval, but he wanted to bask in it, to remain in it, to please the One who took pleasure in him.

Later, Jesus spoke about the allegiance of approval, telling those who would listen that they *should* fear—but they should fear correctly. Namely, they should not fear the Pharisees. The Pharisees persisted in one big charade of spiritual gatekeeping: *Do this. Don't do that.* They taught slight tweaks on God's law that sounded good and right but in fact turned everything wrong. Everyone feared getting it wrong, feared being denounced by the religious leaders—and therefore, they believed, condemned by God himself.

Jesus spoke up.

"What's the worst they can do?"

I imagine he paused there to let them ponder, because the gatekeepers certainly wielded power over their lives.

"They can take your life, that's the worst they can do. But there is more to life than your physical heart beating. There is the matter of your inner person, the part that lasts eternally. Fear the One who judges the heart, not trembling in insecurity as if God were fickle but in amazement that this God never forgets you. He values you so much that he keeps count of the hairs you've shed this very morning, as a lover memorizes every feature and curve of his beloved."[2]

He sees you, in other words. He doesn't ask for your gaze and then give his to another.

This is the very best news: you don't just give allegiance to King Jesus; you get his allegiance in return! In fact, he went first in setting his gaze upon you, searching for you, and initiating a relationship with you. His allegiance is wholehearted and fixed, steady and true. Because of Christ, he loves you with a love that's called everlasting (Ps. 103:17). He holds you as the apple of his eye (17:8). He envelops you into the unity and fellowship of the Trinity (1 John 1:3). He sustains you (Heb. 1:3) and will not let you out of his sight. The One who holds the gavel of judgment, able to pronounce you either condemned or approved, has declared your unchangeable status as approved (Rom. 8:1). God doesn't just love you; he is *for* you (v. 31).

An allegiance to approval will tell you all kinds of insidious lies contradicting these truths, primary among them that God is not love. He is instead fickle, his love changing according to our performance, and therefore we should constantly be seeking and earning his approval through our words and actions—and therefore his love remains forever out of reach. *His eye may be on the sparrow*, the whispers say, *but his eye is not on me.* Beneath all these lies, we find his love insufficient and of course grab for more from the people around us.

This is what all of life comes down to: not who around you loves you or how well they do so, but rather whether or not you know the love of God *for you* as an absolute and unchanging truth.

When we know this love is sure, something happens to our "need" for the approval of others: it's overpowered like a tsunami wave crashing onto the shore and pulling everything in sight under its weight and authority.

Measure Correctly

I've set this up as a choice between two equals: either choose an allegiance to how others think of you or choose an allegiance to King

Jesus and his love. While there is choice, these are not equal options. We must see the ridiculousness of maintaining our allegiance to the varied and always-changing opinions of others, who themselves have distorted allegiances, when we already rest comfortably within the love of our good God. There is only one love we absolutely need, only one that will fill us to overflowing, and we have it!

The choice, then, is whether we'll battle our false allegiance or excuse ourselves from the fight because it's difficult and often painful to untangle ourselves from the opinions of others.

During times of uncertainty or change, I often revert back to thoughts akin to my old nature. Instead of resting in God's love, I drown in self-condemnation and timidity, especially in relation to other people. I am driven by the self-perceived expectations of others, and they're always unattainable, like giants towering over me with disappointment in their eyes. My need for their love and approval trumps the love the Lord so freely whispers in my ear. In times when I have most needed to reflect on God's love and sovereignty over my life, I have instead looked for assurance from people.

I hate when I find myself once again groveling at the feet of others, eager for any pittance they'll give, but at least I can now recognize when I'm doing it, fight for truth, and confess my misplaced allegiance to the Lord. The fight, however, is ongoing; it's never lessened, it's never gotten easier. In fact, the more I recognize my false allegiance, the more the Holy Spirit points out where my motivations lie, the more specifically painful the fight has become.

But I've definitely learned how best to fight.

First, I must use correct measurements.

This past week we went to the beach, normally a place of fun and relaxation, but my heart roiled in turmoil over the cares of life much like the waves at the shore crashing on repeat. Sitting on the balcony of our rental one morning, I prayed through my unrest as I watched Kyle and our boys playing on the shoreline. From my perch, I looked out at the vast ocean extending far past my line of sight and realized I hadn't yet taken stock of the ocean; I'd spent most of the week on the beach looking down at my kids, helping them look for seashells or chasing crabs. And so, truly seeing it for the first time, I tried to take it all in: the ocean deep, powerful with waves, and yet this slice just a tiny portion of its entirety. It was immense, immeasurable, and I suddenly remembered that God describes his love in similar terms. The measuring stick extends far past any human horizon.

The boys squealed as they rode waves, and I turned my eyes toward them in order to delight in their delight. And they suddenly looked so small. Even my husband, a grown man, was no match for the ocean (or children shooting at him on boogie boards, powered by the waves).

I think of this when I want the approval of others. I love my husband and children, and I of course want to enjoy their love toward me. But what fuels this love, what powers this human love is a greater love, a love as persistent and faithful as the waves hitting the shore. Pursuing the approval of others as our greatest allegiance is like looking for a speck of love while ignoring the tsunami of love around us. We can only be in right relationship with others when we're drenching ourselves in the ocean of God's love. We measure whatever love and approval is given through others as ultimately from the hand of God, and we turn in praise to him.

So we drench ourselves. We measure correctly, and then we continually wash our minds in the refreshing water that is the bedrock truth of God's unassailable love.

For many years, I didn't feel the approval of God. I didn't feel sure of his love for me. I certainly didn't feel secure in it. But when all else failed, when all my crutches were kicked out from under me, I became desperate for truth, and I started to gulp-drink the Bible.

What I discovered is that I couldn't escape God's love. No matter if I was disoriented in Isaiah or at home base in Galatians, the authors hammered and hammered and hammered on God's everlasting love. I found him to be patient, gracious, firm, and extremely committed to his people.

And I started to believe it. I started to believe that, no matter how I felt about myself and no matter how others felt about me, God actually loves me.

But there are later rounds in this fight, because belief always gets tested.

When Saying No Tests Your Allegiance

Nothing tests our resistance of an allegiance toward approval more than saying no to a request or choosing to obey God even if it means disappointing someone's expectations. Where our true allegiance lies, in other words, reveals itself most when we're making decisions about where we'll spend our time, energy, money, and gifts. Will we make decisions according to what God says and the priorities he's clearly given us? Or will we beg for a pittance of love from another, figuratively reciting a love sonnet to God while looking at another?

Of course this means we must first know what our priorities are, and rehearse them over and over in our minds and hearts.

You and I have the same first priority: we are disciples of Jesus. We're students of his—pursuing him, learning him, learning by his Spirit to live as he did.

Beyond that, our priorities likely diverge, depending on where God has placed each of us and in what roles. The point is that our schedules and choices should display our priorities, and throughout life we'll be presented with a myriad of (good) opportunities that don't align with our God-given priorities. What then?

We display our allegiance to Jesus and, more specifically, *our trust of his Spirit's leadership*, when we say no to what he's not prompted us to do.

In order to live this out well, I've learned to be slow in my responses. I know how susceptible I am to saying yes to everything, so I've practiced slowing down and prayerfully considering whether or not an opportunity matches with both my God-given priorities and my current God-given limitations. Most importantly, waiting to give an answer allows space for the Holy Spirit to either ignite passion and excitement regarding the opportunity or to show me any wrong motivations in wanting to say yes.

Saying an actual no to something I want to say yes to from a place of seeking approval sends me into immediate turmoil every single time. I want to please, I want to win admiration, and above all, I don't want to disappoint.

But then I get out my measuring stick. I remember my kids, specks on the beach, contrasted by the ocean.

I remember what love will fulfill me and what love will remain no matter what I do.

I am not a disappointment to God, and so I do not want to disobey him. He is delighted in the leadership and work of his Spirit in my life today,[3] and if he wants me to throw myself fully into an opportunity, he'll let me know.

If I just sit in my unrest while I drench myself in the truth of God's love, eventually the unrest dissolves, and I realize with great joy that I am free as a bird. I'm free from an allegiance to approval, but even more so, I'm free to love people with the time, energy, and gifts I have to give, as my King directs I give them.

When we're free in God's love, we no longer crave the approval of others and can actually love *them*, rather than using them to get love for ourselves.

His Vow of Approval

He was always there. In the skit, I mean. As I traversed the stage, losing my rose petal by petal, our Designated Messiah stood behind me, following me with his eyes.

He watched as I silently pleaded for the approval of others.

He watched as I broke down in tears.

He watched as I fell to my knees in anguish, but I couldn't see him. I couldn't see him standing on a chair, my drama team friends acting as crucifiers, nailing his hands on an invisible cross. I couldn't see him as he rose from his death and moved toward me.

But then he found me, took my pitiful, empty stem and exchanged it with a new white rose. He looked me in the eye and smiled.

I found the love I'd been looking for all along.

It's much like a marriage vow.

Last week Kyle and I went away overnight, and as we always do when we take a step back and view our life together, we marveled at where we've come. We're no longer young newlyweds, and the process of becoming not young has been a harrowing journey. There have been hard-won lessons and hard-fought victories, and there have most certainly been tears. There is only one explanation for how we've made it through some of our darkest days intact: there is a God, and he's carried us.

Driving home, watching the bare trees blurring into gray outside my car window, I thought about our wedding day and the vows I made to Kyle. I vowed to be faithful, and I meant it, and I have been, but I was so incredibly young when we married; I really had no idea what it would take to fulfill my promises. I had no idea the labels I'd have to let go or stop pursuing in order to love and be loved.

I thought then about what faithfulness is, and how a steadfast marriage is a picture of a greater reality of God's faithfulness.

Because sometimes I feel as if I'm shouldering the world. When I think ahead to what needs to be done, or when I consider what others within my reach need, or when I wonder how I can make the future unfold in just the way I'd like, I feel the heavy weight of my desired wholeheartedness to the One who has loved me.

This is me, playing God again, attempting to pick up precisely what he says I should cast upon him.

I'm learning, however slowly, to be human, and part of the learning is accepting that God himself is not impatient with my humanness.

Because I certainly am.

But God vowed his faithfulness to me long before I gave myself to him, and the treasure of this brings me such comfort. When I consider where I've come in this life, I know I've only been able to remain faithful because he is faithful. He's held me up and together. He's upheld me when I in my weakness couldn't hold on to anything.

The seams of my self—the self-righteousness, self-preservation, self-focus—have burst open within the past year, and it's been as painful as it sounds. But it's been the sort of pain that's like a high fever burning off what harms the body; it's the good pain of sanctification burning off death—a purposeful release of false loves and lifeless labels—precisely so life might flourish.

God's motion has felt slow at times, but then his conviction comes like a driving rain of kindness, and in those times I haven't been able to capture all the truth and grace and hold it together as one. I find myself wanting to "get it," to learn the lesson, complete the assignment, move onward and upward.

And there it is again, the humanness like a prison cell, my frantic turning of the key of self-ability as my supposed way out.

However, when I consider the present moment, my humanness so real and constricting, I remember that he is faithful. He will always be faithful to lead me, help me, and move in me, because this is who he is. No matter how weak or frail I feel in my faithfulness to him, he is delighted in the current working of the Spirit in me.

My life is not dependent upon my own faithfulness to love God wholeheartedly.

It's dependent upon his, and this is what it means to be a Christian, that his vow of love came before mine (Rom. 5:8).

When I know this love, it shaves my allegiances down to one: to King Jesus alone.

practicing THE kingdom OF god

Below I've suggested some daily practices that God may use to turn your pleading eyes away from others and toward God's love. Remember, it is not the actual practice that will transform you but rather the Holy Spirit who transforms you. Look for him, listen for him in Scripture, and follow his lead.

1. My beggar's sign says, "Will work for love." Consider what your sign might say: "Will _____ for love." How is this action or choice self-protective? What exactly are you attempting to gain from others? How does this action or choice sit as a foundational motivation for the way you live your life? Ask God to make you aware of this motivation, and spend the next week taking note of just how much it's infiltrated your life.

2. What are your unmet desires? What labels do you seek? If you got them, can you imagine that there would be difficulties that come along with it?

3. On whom have you specifically set your pleading eyes? Imagine that they give you what you've always hoped they would. Would that love satisfy you forever?

4. Dwell on the fact that Jesus experienced the disapproval and rejection of others. What does that mean to you? How does that knowledge help you choose obedience over the approval of others?

5. Practice turning your eyes toward God each day by searching the Scriptures for the absolute truth of his love. Here are some passages to get you started: Romans 8:1, Romans 8:15–17, Romans 8:31–39, 1 John 3:16, and 1 John 4:9–10.

6. Enact the "we" of the kingdom. If you are consistently struggling with an allegiance to approval, confess your sin to someone who will offer you wise counsel and biblical truth. Talk with others about God-given priorities. What are yours? What are theirs? How can you support one another to pursue those, to the exclusion of what God is not leading you to do? Share how you've learned to recognize the Holy Spirit's leading regarding your decisions, and how you've learned to say a joyful yes and a God-honoring no.

7. Often what we have a tendency toward in misplaced allegiance has, at its root, a clue about how God has made us. A person tending toward approval is perhaps a person who rightly desires intimacy and relationship with others. With properly aligned allegiance, this is a person who displays the fruit of love that can only come from the Holy Spirit. Ask him to grow this fruit in you. And consider: How might God, if you live submitted to him, use you and your Spirit-gifted love in his kingdom?

8. For further reading: Galatians 1:10 and 2 Corinthians 3:4.

ELEVEN

comfort

After a few hours at a party, standing in the middle of a room full of people, I know I've reached my full introvert saturation point when my ears begin rattling from the noise of the dozens of conversations happening simultaneously around me and I'm unable to focus on the one I'm currently limping through. And it's also abundantly clear when I begin calculating the size of the gauntlet—How many people must I politely talk with before I can extract myself from this situation? If I've noticed my saturation, it's quite possibly too late for the "polite" part, and so I begin the internal pep talk.

Just think! You'll soon be home, under the covers, disappearing into a good book. In total silence.

I smile and nod at my conversation partner while covertly scanning the room for my husband. Locking eyes with Kyle, I give him the signal and we begin moving through the room together, partners in a secret dance only introverts know. We say our politest goodbyes and our sincerest thanks, we close the door behind us, and I sigh deeply as I nestle into Kyle's side.

I extroverted hard—and gladly so—but now home is in sight, and I am so happy about it.

Pursuing the Good Life

That sort of moment is what I think of when I think of comfort: relief, a state of ease and satisfaction, a deep sense of peace and contentment. And the place I equate most with comfort is my home—the one place on this earth where I've curated, created, and cultivated an existence that both reflects and suits my family and me. Here I am most fully myself and am blessedly at rest, especially when my children are asleep in their beds and the demands of the day have been met. I put up my feet, have an uninterrupted conversation with Kyle, and perhaps watch a show or two.

This is often my goal, the reward I promise myself when I'm taxiing children from one activity to the next or when I'm volunteering my time to others. If the task is especially taxing, I simply imagine myself sitting on the couch at the end of the day with a completed checklist to show for myself, ingesting a small dessert as my earned treat.

There are moments, however, when I'm lost in both my sugary sweets and my sugary television show and I recognize I haven't actually found comfort in what I've rewarded myself with. Tomorrow and its cares already loom in my mind, exhaustion presses down on me, and the sweet treat has been consumed in a fleeting minute. I feel as if I'm trying desperately to sink down into a figurative couch of ease, enveloped in a cozy blanket, but I can't get comfortable. I can't find the end of my sinking. I cannot truly find the sense of peace I seek.

It's in these moments of awareness that I recognize my allegiance has turned once again toward my own comfort. I'm not just interested in my own comfort; I'm *adamant* in pursuit of it, believing I've earned ease, believing because of my devotion to him that God owes me a comfortable life, even believing God's *promised* me this.

When I unravel why I can't find peace, I find all sorts of lies tangled up together, chief among them that God is not who he says he is. He is not the God of all comfort (2 Cor. 1:3), the Prince of Peace (Isa. 9:6), or a rewarder of those who seek him (Heb. 11:6). He is instead a killjoy, a demander, a taskmaster, and a taker rather than a giver, so I'll snatch whatever fleeting comfort I can get out of this life, thank you very much. If I can't be confident that God will bless me, I'll just go ahead and bless myself.

That's what this is about, really: we're after the good life. We think the good life is smooth sailing on a luxurious vessel, and we believe the good life is *earned*.

An allegiance to King Comfort, therefore, is ultimately an allegiance to reward.

We face this temptation in countless forms without even realizing it. Our allegiance to comfort branches out into jealousy, envy, bitterness, passivity, spiritual temper tantrums, works-based religion, greed, and laziness. We would rather revel in what comfort we do have than risk trusting God. We instead look to cultural cues for what our lives *should* look like: we should be married, tucked away in a home with granite countertops, birthing children who excel at life and who, when grown, do what we want them to do while living where we want them to live. We genuflect before family, relationships, country, and bank accounts, begging them to provide our security.

These are good things, are they not? Family, relationships, country, money? God gives these gifts to his children, placing us in families, giving us what we need and even sometimes what we want. But if we don't consistently trace the hands holding the gift back to the Gift-giver himself, we'll develop such a fear and dread of *not* having those gifts in the future that we'll form an idolatrous attachment to good things and find ourselves wholly unable to actually enjoy them.

False allegiances, as we've repeatedly discovered, always blur our vision and offer life while giving death. With an allegiance to comfort, we typically have a misunderstanding of what the good life actually is and where it's to be found.

In order to parse this misunderstanding, we must first ask ourselves, Is comfort God's goal in the Christian's life?

In Scripture, a life of ease is often equated with complacency. The prophet Isaiah specifically warned the Israelite women who lounged around, unthinking, to "rise up" and pay attention to their spiritual state (Isa. 32:9–20). They'd become immune to injustices playing out around them and complacent to the needs of others. This complacency had grown among them like weeds in a garden because they were financially prosperous yet inattentive to God. They were reveling, entitled, in their "reward" and didn't yet realize how the weeds were already choking out their spiritual vitality.

If comfort is our ultimate goal, as it was for the Israelite women, we will forever shrink back, never taking risks that require faith and entirely missing the *actual* good life that Jesus described as the abundant life.

There is no stasis for the Christian. We're certainly given God's comforting presence in the person of the Holy Spirit, but his comfort is always meant to *move* us rather than *settle* us further into ourselves.

Take, for example, a verse I mentioned previously describing God as the God of all comfort. Let's read it in context: "Blessed be the God and Father of our Lord Jesus Christ, the Father of mercies and God of all comfort, who comforts us in all our affliction, so that we may be able to comfort those who are in any affliction" (2 Cor. 1:3–4).

This passage assumes both affliction and movement.

Notice the "so that." God gives us his comforting presence so we will know and trust him in our discomfort, *so that* we'll move toward others who are facing discomfort with his name on our lips.

We can definitively know that God's goal for the Christian is not a life of ease. If we desire this, we don't desire the kingdom of God as it is. If your god doesn't ever require anything uncomfortable from you, you have an allegiance not to him but to your own comfort.

You are the god leading your life, not the God of the Bible, and your life is likely characterized by a constant falling back, a retreating, a self-protective mentality.

You and I must know that the God of the Bible doesn't call us to pursue the good life; he calls us to pursue the *abundant* life.

And the abundant life comes through both holy discomfort and holy risk.

Holy Discomfort

In Isaiah 32, the prophet describes fruitful vineyards and pleasant fields coming to ruin because those who are at ease are inattentive and apathetic toward God. Isaiah calls those who lounge inside their homes to go outside and tend their fields. They are to pluck weeds and thorns from the soil of their hearts so righteous fruit will grow.

Jesus uses similar agricultural analogies when he describes the kingdom of God and our place in it. He said his kingdom is much like a tiny, seemingly insignificant mustard seed, which when sown into a field grows into a tree far surpassing its humble beginning. Locating himself in the kingdom, Jesus identifies himself as a farmer who casts seed into various types of soil and his Father as a vinedresser who prunes and cultivates within the vineyard.

Where are we in this picture? We are the soil—hopefully the good soil Jesus described, ready receptacles for the seeds of truth—and we're also the plant that grows and bears fruit. Together, we're a crop soon ready for harvest.

My brother-in-law Travis is a farmer, and he daily dips his hands in the fertile south Texas soil that is his family's very provision. In the winter, the realized hope of summer harvest has passed, the remnants of harvested crops have been destroyed, and the soil he sifts in his hands has once again taken center stage. He has already turned, tilled, leveled, and molded the soil into neat rows and borders, preparing ready receptacles for seeds. February days are for fertilizing—acres and acres must be covered, and then acres and acres must be planted with various species of seeds: sorghum, sugar cane, cotton, sesame, or cabbage.

His work—the daily wrestling with the soil—is circadian and perennial yet has only ever just begun. After planting, he will scrupulously monitor the soil, coaxing it with aeration, searching it for even the smallest of weeds, scrutinizing it for signs of pests or worms. And then he will wait, giving time and space for the sun and the rain and the mysterious and miraculous work of seeds becoming sprouts becoming stalks.

Travis is whom I think of as Jesus draws our attention to the seed, soil, and farmer, and I imagine myself as the one cultivated. Just as Travis meticulously works his land, God carefully and continuously works in me. At my rebirth a seed of life sprouted, watered by the Holy Spirit, and I began growing up toward the sunlight. At some point, I noticed a certain kind of love and joy welling up in me that I had not chosen but seemed to have chosen me.

Jesus said it would be like this:

> The kingdom of God is as if a man should scatter seed on the ground. He sleeps and rises night and day, and the seed sprouts and grows; *he knows not how*. The earth produces by itself, first the blade, then the ear, then the full grain in the ear. (Mark 4:26–28, emphasis mine)

Fruit came, and I didn't know exactly how the Holy Spirit produced it, only that mysterious elements were at work over time.

I've noticed something else, however: the fruit didn't come without painful pruning.

Holy discomfort is a constant in the Christian's life as the Holy Spirit upends the soil of our hearts, yanks out weeds, and begins a new work in a new field with a different sort of seed. Cyclically, perennially, he doesn't let us remain fallow or fruitless because he has our full maturity in mind.

Here I sit in middle age, halfway between where I began and where I, God willing, have yet to go. I'm no longer a seed but a plant. But I often find myself spiritually tired. That is to say, I grow easily frustrated at myself for not being further along in my growth. I am weary in the battle against my own flesh. Tears come easily when I think of the day when God will bring me in with the harvest, when I'll be done submitting to the constant tilling, pruning, and the giving of the fruit's seed for more planting.

That will be the day of ease, but for now I am meant for holy discomfort.

And God is completing the good work he began in me with that small seed of life.

In other words, life and fruit grow through holy discomfort.

Holy Risk

The abundant life also grows through holy risk.

Interestingly enough, as Jesus's ministry expanded, he began removing himself from the agricultural analogy and instead inserting his listeners in his stories, casting his followers in the farmer's role. He foreshadowed the time when he'd physically leave and send his Spirit to reside in them. He pointed to the crops: "Open your eyes and look at the fields! They are ripe for harvest" (see John 4:35). He of course wasn't telling the disciples to gather the grain. He was telling them who they were to be: cultivators. They were to work the plot of land God had assigned them.

I think again of Travis. A farmer, perhaps more than most, knows something about faith and how it is holy risk.

Farming is backbreaking work, dirty work, detailed work, and, most of all, *risky* work. There aren't any guarantees. A few years ago, Travis reminds me, when the crop stood beautiful and bountiful in the fields, ready for harvest, a hurricane blew through the Rio Grande Valley and wiped it away entirely. All that labor, all that grime, all that waiting—for nothing.

It's no wonder Jesus employs the farmer as an example, nor that Paul uses similar analogies, telling Timothy to be strong in the grace of Christ by pointing specifically toward the hardworking farmer (2 Tim. 2:6). When he exhorts the Galatian churches toward endurance, he speaks of perennial planting and patiently waiting for an inevitable harvest (Gal. 6:9).

What is the point? Why would we invest everything in a risky venture? We might ask this, thinking of our own lives of faith and our own efforts to produce a spiritual harvest that have seemingly harvested nothing or been wiped out entirely.

The farmer looks at his failed crop as a tangible reminder that the harvest inevitably belongs to the Lord. The farmer must be faithful to lay the groundwork for the harvest, but the harvest cannot be forced; it can only happen through the Lord's providence.

Travis tells me of his cautious optimism as the harvest approaches each year, how at the last minute the weather can change and how there is nothing he can do to protect his crop. He draws the connection for me to the Christian life:

> It's like parenting. I'm parenting my kids over a long period of time, and there are little moments that show me I'm on the right track, but I know I won't see the full reward until the end. Even then, I may not see the reward that I want to see. As in farming, however, there are steps you have to faithfully take to get to the harvest. There are things that pop up in the growing season that aren't helpful or what you want to see. We get rain that we don't want on the crops. I've learned not to go look at the crops on the day it rains, because that's when it looks the worst. It's never as bad as we thought after we come through it, though, and, even what doesn't look good is working toward the end goal of the harvest. In the end, no matter what the crop looks like, we can trust God that he's going to take care of us.[1]

To focus on fruitfulness is a frustrating endeavor; to work in faith is all we are asked to do. *This* is the holy risk. Our lives, like the farmer's, are ongoing and filled with various exercises in learning to trust God despite what we can see today.

The difference between physical farming and spiritual farming is that we're guaranteed a crop in spiritual cultivation: "And let us not grow weary of doing good, for in due season we *will* reap, if we do not give up" (Gal. 6:9, emphasis mine).

The crop we get now, in this time, is both in us and outside of us. The Holy Spirit produces love, joy, peace, patience, goodness, kindness, faithfulness, and self-control in our lives—this is true life, my friends. *This is what we're really searching for when we seek comfort.* We're seeking the peace that only God can grow in us as we look to him and submit to him. This is why holy discomfort is worth it.

But we also reap another kind of crop—that of relationships!

Think about what our idea of comfort is. No matter what our individual desires for comfort entail, they are selfish, self-focused, and isolating. Comfort is about protecting ourselves from anything that challenges us. Because comfort is about self, we cannot be both comfortable and loving people at the same time, and our relationships will suffer for it.

So what this means is we are called to get our hands dirty. We're not meant to settle down, isolated inside our own little spiritual "homes"; we're meant to get outside and work the land. And the land Jesus talks about is *people*. We're cast by Jesus in the role of cultivators in the lives of others—serving them, loving them, sharing Jesus with them, learning from them, helping them grow, and learning about God through them and by observing his work in them.

God's goal for the Christian is that we would experience the joy of the harvest, seeing his work in us and in others.

This is holy risk.

Follow the Leader

Sometimes I get tired, though.

My husband and I have been married and in ministry for twenty years. We have parented for nearly seventeen years, with six more years of intense parenting left to go. We've completed just over a decade of planting and growing a church, and I'm staring ahead at years of more cultivating, weeding, and watering. I often feel like a farmer who has enjoyed a good crop but who is looking at bare fields, preparing to start the planting cycle all over again. At times I feel trapped by the everydayness of life and how much work there is yet to do. I stand with the soil cupped in my hands, wondering if my labor matters or if it will amount to anything in the end.

How do we continue in all God has called us to do without growing weary and giving up, especially when the work is demanding and the harvest appears so far removed?

How do we continue in our holy discomfort and holy risk when we only crave ease and comfort? How do we give our allegiance to a King who himself didn't truly have a home and was wholly unconcerned with creature comforts?

Peeking in on a conversation between Peter and Jesus gives us a clue.

After Peter watched Jesus miraculously feed thousands of people and walk among the adoring crowds, he was riding high. He'd correctly answered Jesus's question concerning his identity as the Son of God, and Jesus had announced he was giving Peter the very keys to the kingdom.

In the next breath, Jesus talks about how he was headed into Jerusalem to face suffering and his own death, and Peter's sense of equilibrium is rocked. He would not hear of it, and he chides Jesus for saying such things.

Jesus's response is telling, not just to Peter but also to us: "You are a hindrance to me. For you are not setting your mind on the things of God, but on the things of man" (Matt. 16:23). Jesus continues, telling Peter what it would look like if he were to set his mind on the things of God. To set your mind on God, he says, means to imitate him—the same One who just announced he was walking right into suffering. He was going to give his life away, allowing himself to be buried as a seed that would bear the incredible fruit of bringing many sons and daughters to glory.

Jesus told them, "If anyone would come after me, let him deny himself and take up his cross and follow me. For whoever would save his life will lose it, but whoever loses his life for my sake will find it" (vv. 24–25).

I think of trying to sink into my couch, sink into comfort. As hard as I try, I can't find its end, and I will eventually lose the life I seek in trying to find it there.

But if I go out and follow in the footsteps of Jesus, walking with him in his vineyard, tending the plot he's given me, I learn to forget myself, because I find life in giving myself away to him. I'm not protected from the elements, and I can't in and of myself make the crop grow, but I am right there where Jesus is.

I get him, and I get to see him at work.

Holy discomfort is not all about work. Sometimes it's uncomfortable to rest, and sometimes it's uncomfortable to cultivate. The point is to walk closely with Jesus. As I follow him, sometimes he leads me to rest beside still waters. Sometimes he asks me to give up rest for the sake of loving others. Sometimes he stops me from planting so the land can recover and I can too. Sometimes he gives me more than I can handle so I will depend on his strength. Sometimes he asks me to pull in the crops and feast, rejoicing.

This is how we keep good things from becoming ultimate things: we eat the good, full of thanksgiving. We enjoy the crop, but the crop fuels us for continued work. We always plant again, the cycle ongoing. We remember that the field belongs to the Lord, and the growth comes "we know not how"—through the mysterious work of the Holy Spirit.

According to Jesus our King, his kingdom requires follow-ship. We follow our King to self-death. We follow him in losing ourselves for the sake of God and others. *But we also follow him to the reward!*

Jesus gives Peter (and us) the reason we'd give up comfort in order to give ourselves away: "For the Son of Man is going to come with his angels in the glory of his Father, and then he will repay each person according to what he has done" (v. 27). I've often read that as, "You'd better get your act together." But Jesus is telling us that God will repay us for what we've lost, what we've intentionally given up, and what we didn't focus on for his sake.

Worker in the harvest, he will give you your life.

Follow Jesus to your reward.

A Guaranteed Reward

An allegiance to comfort is an allegiance to reward.

Jesus doesn't reprimand our allegiance to reward. He does, however, set our minds toward the *real* reward.

Travis tells me that farming is a way of life, a lifelong commitment. It's not a typical job, he says, where you can give your two weeks' notice and walk away. When you farm, you're connected to a specific land and oftentimes to previous generations of your family who have farmed before you, and you've invested in expensive equipment and a community. In other words, there is a deep-roots, big-picture perspective required. The big picture is this: the farmer is covenanted to his or her work for a lifetime, and the land is worked with the yearly harvest ever to come. Every investment in equipment, every decision regarding the precise planting time, every weed uprooted—all of it is done with the harvest in mind.

This reminds me that I too am called to a lifelong commitment to the harvest, and this lifelong commitment is played out in everyday, small acts of devotion. A lifelong commitment entails unrelenting hard work with brief moments of harvest. I've believed the opposite about the Christian life—that short-term hard work would produce an unending harvest. I suppose I prefer a simpler, more glamorous way, but Scripture never portrays the Christian life this way. At its very center is a commitment to self-death, to a deep-root big picture where the goal can never be instant growth, instant fruit, or instant reward but rather a steady pace over the long haul.

I ask Travis if he thinks about the harvest every day. He says most days he does.

"On the days when you're knee-deep in manure?" I ask.

"Yes," he says.

"When the irrigation line bursts?"

"Yes," he says.

"When you're working sunup to sundown in the summer?"

"Yes, especially then. It's the time of the year that we work the hardest, but it's the most satisfying. You've made it another year; you've grown another crop. It's financially rewarding, but it's also the satisfaction of knowing that you've put it into the ground and you've harvested it."

The reward is always in sight. There is joy in the harvest, and the greatest satisfaction belongs to the one who carefully cultivated it all along the way. The hardworking farmer, as Paul says in 2 Timothy 2:6, "ought to have the first share of the crops." I've taken that to mean that the farmer eats off his labor, but, in talking to Travis, I see that it means so much more.

Joy results from his long-term faithfulness. He is content in his work and in seeing what it's produced over the years. He has learned the secret joy of trusting in God's providence and experiencing his constant goodness. But there is also joy for Travis in what he cannot see. He explains how one tiny seed becomes a huge plant that produces a thousandfold seeds. The harvest multiplies itself and goes out into the world in a way that he will never see with his own eyes. *But just because he can't see it doesn't mean it isn't happening.*

In our work and in our weariness, let us look to the farmer. Let us keep the deep-root, big picture in mind. Let us be vigilant over our present crop, let us rely on others, and let us seek faithfulness above all else. If we don't give up, one day we will enjoy the final harvest and its bountiful rewards. Unlike those of our farming friends, this harvest, one cultivated by faith, is *absolutely guaranteed.*

And we will rest from our work in true comfort, finally called into our forever home.

practicing THE *kingdom* OF *god*

We turn now to a few suggested daily practices that God may use in your life to wither your allegiance to comfort and replace it with faithful cultivation for Jesus's sake. Remember, it is not the actual practice that will transform you but rather the Holy Spirit who transforms you. Look for him, listen for him in Scripture, and follow his lead.

1. What comforts do you often reward yourself with? Are these wrong or necessarily bad? How can we interact with good things without developing idolatrous attachments to them?

2. With properly aligned allegiance, we become people who display the fruit of faithfulness that can only come from

the Holy Spirit. Ask him to grow this fruit in you. And consider: How might God, if you live submitted to him, use you and your Spirit-gifted faithfulness in his kingdom? More specifically, what specific "plot of land" is God asking you to faithfully cultivate?

3. As I spoke to Travis about farming, it struck me how much he mentioned his surrounding farming community. He spoke of relying on his dad and uncles, who have more farming experience; he spoke of relying on common farming knowledge that's been passed down through generations; and he spoke of relying on the larger farming community: "When you don't know what to do, if you ask around, someone is going to help you out." A little jolt of recognition goes through me: "Therefore, since we are surrounded by so great a cloud of witnesses . . . let us run with endurance" (Heb. 12:1). The faith-filled life, like the farming life, must be lived communally. If we are to endure, we will only endure with the help, advice, and companionship of others who are trying to be faithful. Oh, how we need one another! Where are you struggling in your life currently? Are you willing to learn from those who've gone before you? Who can you go to in your church community for help?

4. For further reading: Psalm 126; Hebrews 11:6, 13–16; 1 Corinthians 9:24–27; and 1 Peter 1:3–5.

PART THREE

an unshakeable kingdom

TWELVE

to kingdom come

Since moving to the East Coast, I've become hyperaware of nature's seasons.

In the transitions between seasons, when the calendar begins its countdown, I stand vigil, searching for even the smallest signs of change.

In the height of the heat and humidity of summer, I anticipate the feel of crisp fall mornings, when the sounds of the cars whipping by on the highway near our house inexplicably carry farther and when socks again become necessary.

In the fall, I obsessively circle one specific tree in the school carline, watching as its green bleeds more and more into bright orange each day, and I think of how, though it's beautiful, I'm standing vigil over death. I think of how winter, unseen for now, marches silently toward the horizon, coming for me and for everyone else.

The falling leaves will soon be swept away by November rakes or December winds. Winter, barren and cold, long and harsh, comes. A sense of dread grows in me with each acrobatic leaf leaping off its summer home, for winter always seems the longest waiting.

Its days are short and dark, and I almost forget the light.

Winter, the desperate vigil, the season when I stand at the window, longing for the sun.

Life is full of watching and waiting: for change, for transition, for the dawn of morning after the fear and doubt of darkness.

We've been taught that this search for what's next is somehow wrong, labeling it *discontentment* and scolding ourselves to remain in the present moment. But isn't it so hard to see clearly in the present moment? When we're knee deep in winter's snow or awake in the dark of night, doesn't it warm us even to consider that the day will again return when we will walk barefoot in the grass or sit in the morning sun?

We tell ourselves unhelpful tales of how all restlessness is to be resisted and that all searching is shot through with sin. Certainly, some is. If we set out to seek our peace far from the King and his kingdom, we are on a death march. But sometimes the restlessness announces we're on a fruitless mission and invites us to change course.

I remember being a young mother, chasing a toddler around whom I prayed would look me in the eye and speak a word, any word, and how as I prayed, I cried and cried and cried. Tears were constant, and I felt as if I were stumbling through middle-of-the-night darkness.

I'd always lived with hope for the future, but then, suddenly, the future appeared like a thunderstorm in the distance and my sunny hopes disappeared behind looming clouds. In all my blue sky, bright sun days, I'd never considered that the future might hold hard things, hard things that don't go away.

As my tears poured, I realized my hope for the future—the tales I'd told myself—hadn't been real but rather something like a vapor. My hope had been carried along upon human ideas and human plans and a human agenda. And no human agenda writes pain into the plan. No one wishes to be shattered, but that shattering showed me how I'd given my heart to a breakable, decaying kingdom.

My tears were bitter as I swallowed them and as they trickled down onto my wet pillow, because the hope and joy had gone away. Or perhaps it was clear then how my hope had been in myself all along, with a little Jesus sprinkled on top.

What's difficult is when there are no signs of change, when the darkness continues on without end and living in the present feels mute and barren. Living in the present means only more tears. *Strength* for the present is more of what we need, for we cannot notice enough to actually see; we only see blurrily through our tears. It's a comfort then that Jesus teaches us to pray, "Give us this day our daily bread," for he knew we'd need in this present day strength to walk not in sight (or strength simply to raise the blinds and let the day in at all) but rather in faith, believing in what's come before and what he said will come still.

Living in the present is right and good, and we should take notice of as much as we can take in, but our restlessness teaches us more than that. We must also live in the past, looking back, taking notes, and remembering how the daily bread has been given before. When I can't sleep and the anxious thoughts come in the dark, I remember what I know is sure: the dawn is coming.

And if the dawn is steady and true, what shall we say about its Maker?

In those years when I cried and cried and cried, I began to be glad. I wasn't glad for my present circumstances, not one single bit. I was glad, however, that my own heart had been revealed to me and all the hopes I'd so carefully crafted were ripped out at the roots. I was glad to be shown the breakable kingdom, because it dissatisfied me and always had, and my restlessness led me to my true hope: King Jesus. He was and is in the pain and difficulty, pulling the eyes of my heart forward, teaching me to live for the dawn.

Because the future belongs to him. The future is an unshakeable kingdom.

To see this is to see the sun when I close my eyes in darkness. To see this clearly is a weapon in my hands, fighting against whatever comes with the intent of dividing and shattering my heart. For "temptation only works if the possible futures open to [us] are concealed."[1]

The possible future—no, the *sure* future—shatters the shattering forces and makes us wholehearted before our King.

Assured of the Future

As we've previously discovered, the kingdom of God has already come, manifested and proclaimed by Jesus Christ the King. But the plan for and inauguration of this kingdom began long before the coming of Christ. It was spoken of first as Adam and Eve were banished from Eden, clearly promised by God to King David, and prophesied by God's spokespeople to a divided and conquered people wracked by their sin. Jesus came to prove, by conquering sin and death, the power of God over all other authorities competing for the throne. He was the first to open the womb of the grave, and he passed through death to life with an extended hand as invitation for others to follow. This is what it means that the kingdom of God has come: Jesus has exercised and is exercising his rule and reign in the hearts of those who profess allegiance to him.

The kingdom of God is also now. If we are in Christ, we're considered citizens of a heavenly kingdom we've yet to enter (Col. 1:13; 2 Pet. 1:11). We, however, continue living among the ruins of the earthly kingdom, one temporarily affected by spiritual forces of evil and demonic working through Satan's sons of disobedience (Eph. 6:12; 2:2). We have yet to experience the fullness of Christ's reign. The kingdom of God is thus currently hidden in plain sight, a seed buried in the hearts of those who are his, made visible and tangible and active when those who are his gather together. God is presently acting among humanity through his Spirit's work to relieve them from bondage to Satan and to this, his earthly kingdom. In other words, the kingdom of God is visible when we joyfully subject ourselves, individually and together, to the rule and reign of Christ. We are ambassadors and outposts of a kingdom we know now only by heart.

So the kingdom of God has come and is present now, but it's also yet to come. While on earth, Jesus promised he'd come again and bring the full blessedness of the kingdom with him for those who are his. We have only a taste now (Heb. 6:4–5), but one day we will visibly see and experience Jesus disposing of evil and arraying his full power and glory. One day we will see him whom we love! At that moment, every knee will bow and every tongue confess that Jesus is Lord, because they will see with their eyes that his rule and reign extend over all people and all creation. The kingdom will come in all its perfection and joy, and the King will reign without warring factions attempting to topple his throne. *We will finally be wholehearted before King Jesus.*

Do you think about what this will be like? Do you consider what the full blessedness of the kingdom will mean for you? Do you imagine this for the reality it will be?

We must.

We must know our future and think about, dwell on, and dream of it so that when we cry and cry and cry, we know the hope of the day when morning will dawn and all tears will stop.

We must know our future so that, when we suffer, we know with great assurance that the weight of our future glory is vastly out of balance with our pain; so that when we experience broken relationships, we imagine their eventual restoration and are willing to work now for what will be true later; so that when we toil, we know we will reap the fruit of our faithfulness if we do not give up; so that when we consider bowing to a false king, we remember where all of existence is headed and how that false king will be exposed and discredited before Jesus.

The Bible tells us what we can know about our future:

The kingdom of heaven will be diverse, though singular in focus.

"When the Son of Man comes in his glory, and all the angels with him, then he will sit on his glorious throne. Before him will be gathered all the nations" (Matt. 25:31–32).

Around that throne will be people from all races, tribes, languages, and nationalities, having all things in common because all will worship Jesus.

The kingdom of heaven is our inheritance.

"Then the King will say to those on his right, 'Come, you who are blessed by my Father, inherit the kingdom prepared for you from the foundation of the world'" (v. 34).

The kingdom of heaven doesn't hold a place for sin and death.

"Then comes the end, when [Christ] delivers the kingdom to God the Father after destroying every rule and every authority and power. For he must reign until he has put all his enemies under his feet. The last enemy to be destroyed is death" (1 Cor. 15:24–26).

Jesus will destroy what makes us hide from him and keeps us from one another: anxiety, the validation we seek from others, greed, pride, isolation, selfishness, and self-protectiveness. What hurts us, and what we do that hurts others—banished. Our idols will be exposed and will no longer tempt us, and the death that swallows us all will be forgotten entirely.

In the kingdom of heaven, we will reign over the new earth with Jesus.

"[The saints] sang a new song, saying, 'Worthy are you to take the scroll and to open its seals, for you were slain,

and by your blood you ransomed people for God from
every tribe and language and people and nation, and you
have made them a kingdom and priests to our God, and
they shall reign on earth" (Rev. 5:9–10).

The kingdom of heaven is an unshakeable kingdom.

This kingdom is "an inheritance that is imperishable, un-
defiled, and unfading" (1 Pet. 1:4).

Though it's difficult to imagine in our present darkness, it is our
sure future.

The dawn *will* come.

Prepare Yourself for the Kingdom of Heaven

As his life on earth drew to a close, Jesus began changing his terms
in order to tell us about this future.

In the beginning of his ministry, he proclaimed the kingdom of
God. This kingdom, he said, is open to anyone who would come,
and he invited people in through the Door—himself. He contrasted
this supernatural kingdom with the earthly one we instinctively
know, showing how the kingdom of God consists of the meek and
poor in spirit rather than the religious and prideful.

But then he began referring not to the kingdom of God but
rather the kingdom of *heaven*. He drew his audience's eyes forward
to understand what only their hearts could see, and he told parables
to orient us toward the future kingdom in our everyday lives.

In other words, he said we should close our eyes in the middle
of the night and know the sun will rise in the morning. We should
not only anticipate the dawn but also prepare for it.

The time my family and I prepare most for what we can't yet see is
when we're anticipating the arrival of spring. When the grass greens
and the trees bud, my husband hangs the hummingbird feeder from
the porch and waits expectantly for our buzzing friends' return from

their long trip south. I drag the patio furniture from storage, imagining the warm summer nights we'll spend outside, watching the boys catch fireflies in mason jars. We power wash the siding, ridding the house of winter's traces. My youngest son, salivating at the thought of his favorite fruit, reminds me the strawberries will soon be ripe once again and begs that we schedule a trek to the local orchard. On Saturdays, the lawn mowers around the neighborhood come alive in military unison. The dormant city, in other words, awakens with the anticipation of beautiful weather and long, lazy days.

To anticipate is to prepare, and to prepare is to anticipate. Preparation is an eager, joyful awaiting of what's to come; it's saying, "I'm ready! Bring it on!"

This is the type of anticipation Jesus referenced when he spoke of the kingdom of heaven. He knew we'd struggle to wrap our minds around the kingdom, so he spoke in digestible parables, each one wrapped in urgent and eager invitation: *RSVP.*

Come.

Join in!

I imagine he paused for emphasis, catching every eye, before he told some of his last parables, which could be summed up in two words: *be prepared.* For though the kingdom of heaven will show signs before it arrives, it will arrive unexpectedly, like a knock at the door in the night.

Jesus said,

The kingdom of heaven will be like ten virgins who took their lamps and went to meet the bridegroom. Five of them were foolish, and five were wise. For when the foolish took their lamps, they took no oil with them, but the wise took flasks of oil with their lamps. As the bridegroom was delayed, they all became drowsy and slept. But at midnight there was a cry, "Here is the bridegroom! Come out to meet him." Then all those virgins rose and trimmed their lamps. And the foolish said to the wise, "Give us some of your oil, for our lamps are going out." But the wise answered, saying, "Since there will not be enough for us and for you, go rather to the dealers and buy for yourselves." And while they were going to buy, the bridegroom came, and those who were ready went in with him to the marriage feast, and the door was shut. Afterward the other virgins came also, saying, "Lord, lord, open to us." But he answered, "Truly, I say to you, I do not know you." Watch therefore, for you know neither the day nor the hour. (Matt. 25:1–13)

We're told to be the wise ones who are prepared for Jesus's coming. How can we be wise?

And again Jesus spoke to them in parables, saying, "The kingdom of heaven may be compared to a king who gave a wedding feast for his son, and sent his servants to call those who were invited to the wedding feast, but they would not come. Again he sent other servants, saying, "Tell those who are invited, 'See, I have prepared my dinner, my oxen and my fat calves have been slaughtered, and everything is ready. Come to the wedding feast.'" But they paid no attention and went off, one to his farm, another to his business, while the rest seized his servants, treated them shamefully, and killed them. The king was angry, and he sent his troops and destroyed those murderers and burned their city. Then he said to his servants, "The wedding feast is ready, but those invited were not worthy. Go therefore to the main roads and invite to the wedding feast as many as you find." And those servants went out into the roads and gathered all whom they found, both bad and good. So the wedding hall was filled with guests. (22:1–10)

We accept the invitation Jesus gives before the doors to the wedding feast are closed, because the kingdom of heaven will be inaugurated by a sorting. "And he will separate people one from another as a shepherd separates the sheep from the goats. And he will place the sheep on his right, but the goats on the left" (25:32–33).

Those who remain around his throne will have been sorted from those who he's sent away, and this sorting will be based upon one standard: "God judges the secrets of men by Christ Jesus" (Rom. 2:16). We're either in Christ or we're not. We either bow to him or we don't. If we're in him, when we're measured for sorting, we're measured according to his merit before God.

So we turn away from all other allegiances, all other hopes, and we set our minds on the kingdom of heaven, seeing the treasure of who Jesus is. We sell all to buy the One we've found (Matt. 13:44).

Hope and Anticipation of Beauty

I hadn't opened the old shoebox in a decade, but when I lifted the frayed lid, I laughed in delight at the faces of dear friends and family staring back at me. For hours afterward, I sat on my closet floor, poring over stacks of these pictures that held constant vigil for happy college years, newlywed days, long ago ministry events, and first days home with babies.

My heart filled with wonder at being able to see so clearly in the present as I peered into the past. A friendship that began in college through a chance meeting has, in time, grown into one of deep joy and importance. The man who'd become my husband, pictured still very much as a boy, I've seen grow more and more into who God's made him to be. The little baby, the object of several lifetimes of my worry, has now matured and overcome. Looking at time past, I marveled at how the pictures gave me the gift of sight: even in what I could never have imagined becoming beautiful, God had proven himself good.

But then I turned back to my present moment, the very day I was going through old pictures, and I tried to wrap my mind around that day's gifts: the already teenagers and the almost teenager, taking up more space in my home and heart, eating their way through life. I tried to squeeze every ounce of thankfulness from my heart regarding my husband and the state of our union, and I ticked through friends, extended family, our health, the opportunities and influence God's given.

I couldn't enjoy today's moments like I could those of the past, because the present was so difficult to see without fear creeping in. *What if my beloved is taken from me? What if this boy of mine never learns from his mistakes? What if God asks us to say a gospel goodbye to the church we love?* It's as if my heart wanted to protect itself, belying the deeper question at the core of my fear: *What if God isn't actually at work, bringing the kingdom of heaven?*

We're told by our culture, seemingly on repeat, to live in the moment, to be present, and I know there is good in this charge, but living in the present and especially grasping what God is doing in the current moment is like looking in a mirror, dimly (1 Cor. 13:12). We cannot fully see nor can we comprehend the shape of what God is making and the tools he's using to bring all things to the beautiful end of redemption. We can't find out what God has done from beginning to end (Eccles. 3:11), and on a smaller scale we can't grab hold of a present moment with joy unadulterated by sin and darkness. We must not chide ourselves over missing the moments if we can't grab hold of their fullness as they pass.

There is a better way to live in the present. The old box of pictures helps us understand how.

Why are we often more moved by old pictures than new? One reason is that when we look back, those memories are informed by a longer and wider perspective. We're able to view them through the filter of God's goodness, without the fear or uncertainty we might have experienced in the moment, and we can then look forward, trusting God will make similar beauty from the ashes of the hurts and uncertainties in the present.

We see this play out in the life of our King who's gone before us. In the moment of Christ's crucifixion, everything appeared horribly bleak. Now we're able to look back on his death and resurrection and see unparalleled beauty, the kind that fills us with joy. This perspective fuels our hope as we look forward to seeing the promise of his second coming.

Looking back at the past and forward to the future helps us walk by faith in a promise-keeping God in this present darkness. For many of us, both the past and the present are pockmarked with pain. Our hope in this life is set on God's ever-present help and on the reality awaiting us when Jesus sets all things right and all our pain is transformed into glory. Beauty awaits everyone in Christ.

The goal for our present, then, is not grasping the moment as it passes or seeing clearly what God is doing at every turn. The goal for our present moment, though seen dimly for what it is, is faith: believing that God is with us, helping us, working in us, and hurtling us toward a beautiful end.

God has designed us to comprehend and value the true beauty of his work most significantly over time. As an artist pulls the cover off a portrait in a dramatic reveal, as the hiker's perspective of where she's traveled comes into view when she steps onto the mountain peak, one day we will see the scope and beauty of our redemption in full.

More importantly, we'll see God, and in our first awestruck glimpse we'll see the beauty that John, in his Revelation vision, struggled to compare with anything we currently call beautiful. As we take him in, and as we take in a broader horizon of time and God's work in time, our understanding of his beauty will come into far greater focus.

Perhaps then too we will follow the pattern Scripture gives: looking back with eternal eyes, seeing God's goodness in every point of history. A heavenly shoebox of joy waiting for our unending discovery. And what will we look forward to in the future? In heaven, the future is one of joy's eternal increase, every discovery of God's handiwork a new facet of his beauty.

We do not need to see or understand all that God is doing on our hardest days. We just need to know that God is behind this and in this, and that he will make it beautiful in time. We need to know we will one day live and move and have our being in God's unshakable kingdom.

THE *hard work* OF *heart work*

1. How often do you consider and even imagine what the kingdom of heaven will be like? What would it do for your hope and allegiance to Christ to consistently think about the future kingdom?

2. What does it mean that the kingdom you're receiving is unshakeable?

3. What does it mean that the kingdom of heaven is your inheritance? How does that inform whatever false allegiances you continue to cling to?

4. What areas or experiences of your life have been painful and difficult? How can you see, as you reflect on the past, how God has shown his goodness to you specifically in those difficulties? What will this mean for your future in the kingdom of heaven?

5. For further reading: Revelation 21–22 and 1 Corinthians 15:20–28, 42–58.

THIRTEEN

on earth as it is in heaven

We came to do kingdom work.

We came with our car stacked deep, our six-month-old strapped in his car seat, our two-year-old freshly potty trained, and our five-year-old already registered for kindergarten in the school near our new neighborhood.

We unloaded over the next few days, and after the last box was unpacked, I sat on our bed, feeling a mixture of homesickness and uncertainty, and wondered what we were supposed to do next. We'd come to start a church, at the clarion beckoning of God, no less, and just how does one do that, exactly? We'd read the books, we'd raised the money, we'd cast the vision, but no amount of planning can prepare you for the moment you're sitting on your bed in a new city pondering what to do first.

We went.

That's what we did first and second and for many days after that. We went to meet our neighbors, who looked at us like we were aliens when we explained why we'd come. We went to community gatherings and neighborhood meetings and school functions and anywhere the door was open. We talked to everyone who even glanced our way, whether at the park or the Chick-fil-A playground or my son's school. We knocked on doors, and we asked if we could serve.

We asked them to come.

We invited the people we were meeting to our home for Bible study. Few came. But to those who did, we said we were starting a church, and when we envisioned out loud what it could become, it seemed almost laughable to say those things, as if we were children playing pretend. But we kept meeting, we kept forming relationships in the community, and we kept saying those things that sounded laughable even to us: *we're growing a church here.*

Forming a fully established church, we thought to ourselves, is true kingdom work. God must be glad to have us on his side.

But then we went under.

Prior to coming, church planting appeared fairly glamorous in my head. I knew it would be difficult, sure, but I didn't think the difficulty would last long. The reality of the work, however, toppled me much like a wave takes down an unsuspecting beachcomber.

We cried, doubted the original call as being from God, searched for a way out, despaired. We learned quickly that there are no guarantees except God's presence, and that no amount of human effort can change a soul. We learned we were not capable in and of ourselves to do what God had asked of us, and for some reason this felt to me like complete failure.

But we were raised new.

We had nothing left. All that we'd relied on before—crutches of self-sufficiency, structure, and security—were rendered powerless. And that's precisely when we realized church planting hadn't been merely God's call for us to *go* but also God's call for us to *grow*. Faith had been a concept; now faith meant getting out of bed in the morning and *continuing*. Faith meant allowing God to strip us of all our long-held false allegiances—to self most of all—and discovering him worthy of our whole hearts.

We found God to be solid in the uncertainty, insecurity, and daily doubts. We found he is a God who not only calls but helps, meets, provides, empowers, transforms, and gardens. We found partnership in those who'd come with us and those who linked their arms with ours as we continued forward together. It felt as if we'd been born again, awakened to a new understanding of God and what he can do in and through those who trust him.

This is true kingdom work, when God rules and works in our hearts, and we respond with both internal allegiance and external obedience. In doing so, we rest under the umbrella of his protection and blessing. We are his, and he is ours.

We've come this far.

Over ten years later, the vision has become a reality. Our church isn't perfect by any means, but we love it, and God is with us, and he is forming us.

I've looked around on Sunday mornings recently at these people whom I love and it feels like a dream, like someone else ushered this from start to today. And it's true, Someone did.

We did not do this.

I cannot emphasize this enough. We very much just came along for the ride. God asked us to get out of bed each morning, and we kept saying yes.

The tears haven't stopped. The doubting hasn't completely faded. The heartache and the homesickness haven't eased. The work hasn't gotten any easier, and I still fight the temptation to forget God and rely on myself.

But I now know my God. I know he is real and faithful, and I've learned this primarily through the difficulty. So I won't stop. God still asks me to say yes every day, to keep coming to this place where I've lived for over ten years and to keep going as well, and we will.

Because God goes before us.
And I will follow.
Isn't this kingdom work?

Kingdom Work

When we speak of doing kingdom work, it seems we often imagine ourselves as a soldier storming forward into battle or a person in the spotlight on a stage using creative talents or speaking abilities that change the world. We want to do big things for God—and sometimes, if we're honest, for ourselves—and most of the time we'd like it to be a nice, success-oriented mix of both.

As we wait for a future kingdom, it's vital that we consider what it means to live faithfully in this one. What does it mean to do kingdom work? What does it mean to act on our allegiance to Jesus, to live as a citizen of a kingdom we can't yet see? What does it mean to desire the kingdom to come on earth as it is in heaven?

Jesus, as he often did, spoke in parables to help us understand the answers to these questions. He said the kingdom of heaven is like a treasure buried in a field (Matt. 13:44). A man finds the treasure and, exultant in his discovery, sells everything he has in order to buy the field. He releases all his previous holdings and invests his life, future, and well-being in this plot of land. The foundation of his joy is not the land itself but the knowledge of the treasure it contains.

Based upon later parables, we know that Jesus didn't expect this man to live out his days sitting on his investment, waiting for the day the treasure was unveiled for all to see. Instead, the treasure caused him to cultivate the land. Joy leads to cultivation, and cultivation to further joy. He cultivates life because he's found life.

In fact, the land belongs to God (25:14), because all belongs to God. The treasure is Jesus, and we invest ourselves by faith into the treasure and the field—the kingdom and dominion of God.

We become simultaneously a spiritual seed, nurtured and grow-ing, and the workers in the field, nurturing and growing others. We're both receiving and giving away the truth of the kingdom, speaking and showing what this kingdom is like. We extend mercy because he's been merciful. We forgive because he's a forgiver. We love because he first loved us. This is what it means to do kingdom work—that we're cultivators in the specific plot of land we exist in, with the specific talents we've been given (25:14–30).

We act according to our allegiance.

In Luke 17:7–10, Jesus tells yet another parable to help us under-stand what this allegiance looks like in action:

> Will any one of you who has a servant plowing or keeping sheep say to him when he has come in from the field, "Come at once and recline at the table"? Will he not rather say to him, "Prepare sup-per for me, and dress properly, and serve me while I eat and drink, and afterward you will eat and drink"? Does he thank the servant because he did what was commanded? So you also, when you have done all that you were commanded, say, "We are unworthy servants; we have only done what was our duty."

There are two characters in this parable: the master and the ser-vant. The master, of course, is Jesus, and we are his servants.

The parable asks us to consider the master's perspective toward the servant. He does this in order to correct or clarify our per-spective toward our master and toward the work he's called us to as cultivators. He is, in a sense, leading us to look at the servant's *motivation* for service.

First, we must see the master's perspective. He is at home as the workday is coming to an end. The property, fields, or animals the servant has been working with all belong to the master. He is sitting at the table, which indicates his ownership and rest. And because rabbis in biblical times taught from a position of authority, the fact that he's seated at the table he owns indicates clear and definitive authority and lordship.

We peer into the story just as the servant returns to the house at the end of the day. He's been working hard all day, plowing and keeping the sheep. His work at the plow has not been easy, for he's been behind oxen all day, holding up heavy pieces of equipment and stepping in the mud and muck the oxen have left behind. In addition, he's been carefully considering the sheep, as good shepherds must do. In other words, the servant has been faithful, and as he returns to the master's house, he surely comes drained and depleted from the elements and his tasks.

As I read this parable, my thoughts turn quickly to the tasks of cultivating my own field. *Am I a faithful servant?* I often look at my activity with great pride. *Yes, look at all I'm doing. I'm working so hard for my Master.* Or I consider my past obedience. *Look at all I've done. I've worked so hard for my master. Certainly I can come in to my master and revel in the fruit of my labor with him.*

But Jesus doesn't end the parable at the conclusion of the work-day. He takes servanthood into deeper territory, beyond the actual activity and into the heart behind the work. He says the servant has completed a hard day's work and he's come into the house—perhaps for dinner, perhaps to spend time with his family, perhaps to sit and put his feet up. He seems to be done for the day, *but he is greeted with more work.*

This immediately checks my own thinking, for it touches on something deeper than outward obedience. To obey my master with joy—to continue cultivating when so much has already been done—will require a deeper motivation than some sort of checklist or job description.

It will require a personal devotion to my master.

The Master's Response

The master's response to the hardworking servant seems harsh to me. *I think the servant should be able to rest.* Why is the servant not asked to sit and recline at the table with the master?

The fact that the master is sitting is vitally important, because it is a sign of his authority. Jesus is reminding us of "place." God is the owner and authority of the field and therefore determines when it's time to work and when it's time to rest. He's not being harsh with the servant but rather is saying, "Now is not the time to rest." The servant is not invited to a place of equal authority with the master. He is not asked for his perspective on what he will or won't do or what should be expected or not expected.

I think the servant should be thanked, but Jesus makes a point to say the servant is not thanked for having completed the work the master commanded him to do. Again, this seems harsh, but when we compare this parable with the rest of Scripture, we know that God delights in the righteousness and obedience of his children. Certainly, the master in the parable is pleased with the faithfulness of the servant.

However, Jesus says the servant is not considered to have done something special or out of character with who he is. He is a servant, so he serves. Much like we say to our children when they expect a reward for simple chores, "I'm not going to reward you for doing what's expected of you."

Our master asks us for similar obedience. We are servants who serve for the joy of the master. We're not to serve him expecting a reward or favor. We're not to serve him thinking he'll owe us something in return. We're to serve him by cultivating his field because the whole work is his, and we're to seek his purposes and his glory.

We serve to say thank you to the master, not the other way around.

I think the servant shouldn't be given more work. The master, however, gives a final command: "Prepare supper for me, and dress properly, and serve me" (v. 8).

The work continues. The servant, who's been out in the fields among the muck and mess of the ground and the sheep, is now asked to privately and intimately serve the master his meal.

Have you ever prepared a special meal for one person? Perhaps an anniversary or birthday dinner? When I've done so, I took special care to make an elaborate meal and serve it with love. No one else saw or tasted the meal; it was an act of private devotion.

This is the heart of the parable: the master desires service from a well of private devotion. It's as if Jesus is saying to us—the cultivators of his field—"Let it be done for my eyes and for my benefit, not for the eyes of others or for your own benefit. Let our intimate relationship be the reason you do what you do."

What does the servant do?

Does the servant demand some reason for the service?

Does the servant negotiate for something from his service?

Does the servant grumble and complain?

Does the servant selectively obey—working in the fields but not preparing the meal?

Does the servant wait to obey?

Does the servant keep record of his service, believing he's earned merit with the master?

No, the servant recognizes the master's position and his own. He knows who sits in the seat of authority. He recognizes that obedience is his duty because the whole work is the master's work. He recognizes he was created for this. He recognizes the worth of the master. And he serves his master with deep devotion.

In other words, the servant serves.

True Kingdom Work

Throughout this book, we've sought to understand the kingdom of God. We've discovered we have a King, and we've named and rejected pretend kings who seek his rightful place in our hearts.

In other words, we've found our place in the parable of the master and the servant.

We've learned that all comes from the master's hand—and all is also the master's responsibility. The master is inevitably responsible for what happens with his property. He is responsible for providing for all under his dominion. He is responsible for bringing forth the crop in his fields. We, as his servants and subjects, aren't responsible for anything beyond faithful obedience that stems from wholehearted devotion.

This is kingdom work.

What joy this should bring us!

We don't have to worry about doing a great work; we're simply to cultivate a small seed in our small plot of land and leave the rule and results up to God. He gladly takes that responsibility, and as we do when we're responsible for something, the master never actually stops thinking about the work, preparing the work, leading the work, or providing for the work. He appoints days of rest for the servant, but he himself never stops working. Perhaps, then, we could surmise that in the parable Jesus told, the master works harder than the servant.

As I myself consider this truth, thankfulness swells up in me. I will do anything for this master, because he has done, he does, and he will do all for me.

Has it struck you yet who shared this parable, and how he manifested its truths?

Jesus, our King, laid down his crown and became the servant. He submitted to the Father's will, tending the sheep with careful consideration and gentle love. When he served, he was asked to give more. For the joy set before him, he was obedient to his Father, even to the point of death, so that many sons and daughters would be brought to glory with him. He is now seated, resting at the right hand of God, receiving his reward.

But he has not yet begun to celebrate, because he is waiting for us. Remember what the parable said: "*Afterward you will eat and drink*" (v. 8, emphasis mine).

We will one day sit at the table with him as his brothers and sisters, enjoying the rest reserved for the children of God, when the fields will release their harvest one final time.

However, it's not time for that rest. Right now, it's time for work.

It's time for meeting needs.

Doing justice.

Extending mercy.

Speaking truth with grace.

Making peace.

Reconciling.

Creating.

Loving one another.

Storing up treasures in heaven.

Now is the time to give our lives toward joyfully cultivating the seeds of the kingdom.

We set our hearts in devotion upon Christ and serve him all the days of our lives, knowing we will one day be served in the kingdom of heaven.

Run with Endurance

So, my friend, put it down, throw it off—
all the weights you're trying to carry.
You cannot even walk with them, much less run
as you were meant to do.
You've nursed the bitterness, the hidden wounds and words,
the invisibility.
Resentment is too cherished, too familiar,
so you don't see how it drags you down,
how it stops you from the movement you were meant for.

Sin is there, always there, wrapping like tentacles around you,
in your heart,
in your mind,

in your outstretched hands even as you hope for return.
The weights and the sin, though familiar, are indeed enemies
of yours.
At the ankles, they trip.
At the wrists, they bind.
They are familiar but they are able to be thrown off, to
become *unfamiliar.*
Throw them off and run!

For you are in a race.
Look down at the path marked out for you, look down at
the dirt where God has put your feet.
Run!
Look to the right and the left and notice all those who run
beside, urging you to persevere, needing you to help
them persevere.
Run with others!
Look ahead to those who've already finished, calling out to
you with encouragement.
You're in a race, and your work is to run.

The race is not easy.
I know you are weary and faint.
I know you've considered giving up.
I know you've sought a shortcut.
But don't look for a way out.
Instead, look to Jesus, the One who started your feet
running in the first place,
the One who fills your lungs with air and whose blood
pumps in your heart,
the One who ran this very race flawlessly.
He knows what it's like.

He knows the betrayal, the physical suffering,
the wrath of God.
He knows the weight of all your entangling sins,
the hatred, and injustice.

He also knows death,
a death that came through shame and humiliation.
He went further in his knowing
than you will ever know.
He endured
so you yourself can endure
rather than growing heavy with weariness,
drooping down,
unable to move;
rather than growing faint
and giving up.

He ran the race with endurance,
making it possible for you as well.
And His endurance was rewarded
with joy
and honor.

He sets your feet in this path for
future joy and honor
but also for present endurance training,
which results in life and a fruitful crop.

Therefore
lift your drooping hands (look to him).
Strengthen your weak knees (look to him).
Put one foot in front of the other on the path marked out
    for you (look to him).
Subject yourself to the training (look to him).
Let no bitterness grow up and wrap its vines around your
    ankles (look to him).

Because you are on pace
to cross the finish line
and receive the laurels of an *unshakeable kingdom.*

Remember you have a King.

acknowledgments

I've chosen to dedicate this book to my brothers and sisters at Charlottesville Community Church, because my hope is that each of us would worship King Jesus wholeheartedly. I see that he is growing us to do so both individually and corporately more and more, and it makes my heart sing with joy. I love being church with each of you, and I'm specifically thankful for how you love and honor my husband and our children. Being at CCC is one of the greatest privileges of my life!

Specific CCC women helped me with initial concepts for this book and actually (helpfully) steered me away from the direction I had originally intended to go. The theme of the book solidified with the help of Jennifer Agnew, Millie Shipe, Ashley McKinney, Mary Mays, Kristi Carlson, Susan Hamil, Carri Drake, Amy Dodd, Marylyn Kenney, Emily Coleman, Amanda Scott, and Holly Donithan. Thanks to each of you.

Amy, Susan, and Marylyn, as usual, you prayed me through every step of writing this book. I thank God for the gift of friends like you.

Leigh Ellen Barkley, your friendship and specific encouragement in my writing and podcasting have been such a gift. Thank you for using your gift of encouragement on me.

I have the wonderful privilege of connecting with many women online through my blog and podcast. Several of these women have become invaluable cheerleaders and supporters of my work. Thank you, Lan-Vy Ngo and Melissa Smith, for your backing.

Andrew Wolgemuth, you make the publishing side of writing smooth and enjoyable—not an easy feat! I'm grateful to know you have my back and are rooting for my success.

To the team at Baker Books, I'm thankful for the work you do on my behalf. I've loved partnering with you all these years.

To my parents, Larry and Dana Fleming, thank you for being my biggest fans and for your continual support.

My work would not be possible without the constant help and encouragement of my husband, Kyle. Kyle, thank you for making my calling a priority, even when it means more on your plate. And thank you for setting an example for me of what it means to use your gifts and influence to serve rather than building your own kingdom. I respect you so highly.

Will, Reese, and Luke, you are my life's work, and I love watching you grow in wisdom and stature. May you live your lives in allegiance to King Jesus! He is worthy of your all.

To the King of the ages, immortal, invisible, the only God, be honor and glory forever and ever. Amen.

notes

Chapter 2 Behold Your King!

1. The Village Church with Jeremy Treat, "The Cross-Shaped Kingdom," *Knowing Faith* (podcast), April 18, 2018, https://podbay.fm/podcast/1274228164/e/15 24114000.

2. St. Augustine, "Exposition of Psalm 95," *Works of Saint Augustine*, 18:425.

3. George Eldon Ladd, *The Gospel of the Kingdom: Scriptural Studies in the Kingdom of God* (Grand Rapids: Eerdmans, 1959), 47.

4. Nancy Guthrie, "Help Me Teach the Bible: Teaching the Kingdom of God with Russell Moore," The Gospel Coalition, January 11, 2018, https://www.thegospel coalition.org/podcasts/help-me-teach-the-bible/russell-moore-teaching-kingdom -god/.

5. Guthrie, "Help Me Teach the Bible."

Chapter 3 Receiving the Kingdom of God

1. Vaughan Roberts, *God's Big Picture: Tracing the Storyline of the Bible* (Downers Grove, IL: Intervarsity, 2002), 22.

2. I learned about the theological concept of federal headship from my husband, who, along with our church's elders, preached through the book of Romans. The thoughts in this section were first my husband's. I'm indebted to him.

3. I wrote a whole book about my drive toward perfectionism and my struggle to understand grace. It's called *From Good to Grace*, and if you struggle in the same ways, I'd love to come alongside you and share with you what I've learned about the gospel.

4. Roberts, *God's Big Picture*, 43.

5. Ladd, *Gospel of the Kingdom*, 79.

6. Ladd, *Gospel of the Kingdom*, 96.

7. Roberts, *God's Big Picture*, 22.

8. Martyn Lloyd-Jones, *The Kingdom of God* (Wheaton: Crossway, 2010), 208.

Chapter 4 Resisting the Kingdom of Self

1. David Foster Wallace, "Kenyon College Commencement Address," May 21, 2005, https://web.ics.purdue.edu/~drkelly/DFWKenyonAddress2005.pdf, accessed October 23, 2018.

2. The specific interview mentioned here was on how envy affects our relationships. See Christine Hoover with Tilly Dillehay, "Tilly Dillehay on How Envy Affects Our Friendships," *By Faith with Christine Hoover* (podcast), November 21, 2018, http://www.gracecoversme.com/2018/11/tilly-dillehay-on-how-envy-affects-our.html.

3. Russell Moore, *Tempted and Tried: Temptation and Triumph of Christ* (Wheaton: Crossway, 2011), 95.

Chapter 5 Anxiety

1. I understand that *anxiety* is a loaded word, because sometimes anxiety as we define it has purely physiological components, but in other ways we define it we're speaking of spiritual issues. The anxiety I write of in this chapter is anxiety with spiritual roots. I've chosen to use the term because Jesus himself did in the passages I reference, and I use the term interchangeably with *worry*. If you struggle with anxiety and are not sure if it has any physiological roots, I suggest you seek the help of a medical professional and/or biblical counselor. These helps are common graces of God and shouldn't be discounted.

2. Dictionary.com, s.v. "anxiety," accessed July 24, 2019, https://www.dictionary.com/browse/anxiety.

3. Winn Collier, *Love Big, Be Well: Letters to a Small Town Church* (Grand Rapids: Eerdmans, 2017), 24.

Chapter 6 Image

1. I laughed in recognition when I read the great Mo Willems describe this act of protest as "going boneless" in his children's book *Knuffle Bunny* (New York: Hyperion, 2004).

Chapter 7 Control

1. Russ Ramsey, *The Passion of the King of Glory* (Downers Grove, IL: Intervarsity, 2018), 133.

Chapter 8 Escape

1. Mike Tyson, "James Has a Notion Where Blame Belongs," *Los Angeles Times*, August 28, 1987, https://www.latimes.com/archives/la-xpm-1987-08-28-sp-2763-story.html.

2. Neil Postman, *Amusing Ourselves to Death: Public Discourse in the Age of Show Business* (New York: Penguin, 1985), 69–70.

3. Moore, *Tempted and Tried*, 47.

Chapter 9 Isolation

1. I wrote an entire book on the subject of making and cultivating friendships, called *Messy Beautiful Friendship*.

2. Dictionary.com, s.v. "shame," accessed July 30, 2019, https://www.dictionary .com/browse/shame.

3. Ladd, *Gospel of the Kingdom*, 114.

4. Patrick Schreiner, *The Kingdom of God and the Glory of the Cross* (Wheaton: Crossway, 2018), 17. This is a slight variation on Schreiner's definition.

5. Charles Spurgeon, *Morning and Evening* (Wheaton: Crossway, 2003), evening, February 19.

Chapter 10 Approval

1. Steve Kroft, "Tom Brady Talks to Steve Kroft," CBS News, November 4, 2005, https://www.cbsnews.com/news/transcript-tom-brady-part-3/, accessed February 6, 2019.

2. This is my own paraphrase of Luke 12:4–7.

3. This idea was first presented to me by one of our church's preaching elders, Matt Brumbelow.

Chapter 11 Comfort

1. Travis and I have had multiple conversations about farming, but these quotes are from an interview I did with him in February 2016.

Chapter 12 To Kingdom Come

1. Moore, *Tempted and Tried*, 50.

Christine Hoover is a pastor's wife, mom of three boys, host of the *By Faith* podcast, and author of several books, including *Searching for Spring: How God Makes All Things Beautiful in Time*, *Messy Beautiful Friendship*, and *From Good to Grace*. Her work has appeared on *Christianity Today*, The Gospel Coalition, and For the Church. Originally from Texas, Christine and her family live in Charlottesville, Virginia, where they planted a church in 2008. Find her at her home online at ChristineHoover.net.

FOLLOW AUTHOR

Christine Hoover

Connect with Christine at

CHRISTINEHOOVER.NET

#ByFaithPodcast

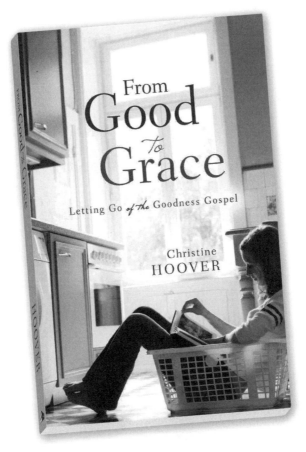

CHASE YOUR LONGING FOR
deep friendships

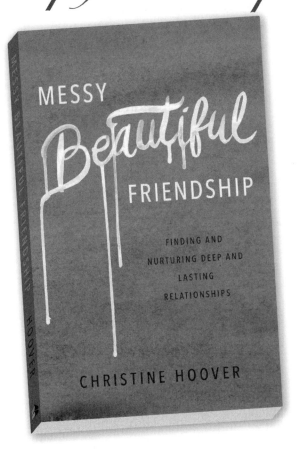

We long for deep and lasting friendships, but they can be challenging to make—and keep. Our expectations of ourselves and our friends can often leave us feeling insecure and isolated. With engaging true stories and guidance drawn from Scripture, Christine Hoover offers a fresh, biblical vision for friendship that allows for the messiness of our lives and the realities of our schedules.

WHEN YOU NEED
HOPE
IN THE DARK OF WINTER

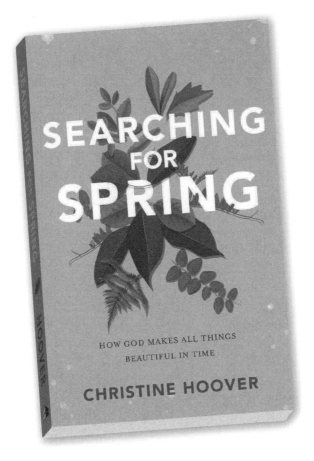

If you are in the midst of suffering, if you find your faith withering, if you are questioning whether God is at work—or even present—as you wait for something in your life to become beautiful, this book will be a welcome reminder that God never stops his redemptive work . . . and that there is a time for everything under heaven.

LIKE THIS BOOK?

Consider sharing it with others!

- Share or mention the book on your social media platforms. Use the hashtag **#WithAllYourHeartBook**.

- Write a book review on your blog or on a retailer site.

- Pick up a copy for friends, family, or anyone who you think would enjoy and be challenged by its message.

- Share this message on **TWITTER**:
  "I loved #WithAllYourHeartBook by @ChristineHoover"

- Share this message on **FACEBOOK**:
  "I loved #WithAllYourHeartBook by @AuthorChristineHoover"

- Share this message on **INSTAGRAM**:
  "I loved #WithAllYourHeartBook by @ChristineHoover98"

- Recommend this book for your book club, workplace, class, or church.

- Follow Baker Books on social media and tell us what you like.

f Facebook.com/ReadBakerBooks

y @ReadBakerBooks